180 Devotions and Worship Activities for Preschoolers

My Best Friend Jesus

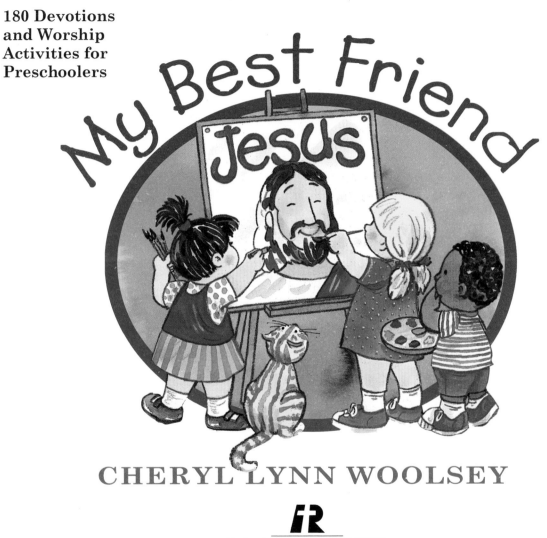

CHERYL LYNN WOOLSEY

REVIEW AND HERALD® PUBLISHING ASSOCIATION
HAGERSTOWN, MD 21740

Credits

Copyright © 1998 by
Review and Herald® Publishing Association
International copyright secured

The author assumes full responsibility for the accuracy of all facts and quotations as cited in this book.

This book was
Edited by Jeannette R. Johnson
Copyedited by James Cavil
Designed by Patricia S. Wegh
Illustrations by Mary Bausman
Typeset: 12/14 Century Schoolbook

PRINTED IN U.S.A.

10 09 08 07 06   5 4 3 2

R&H Cataloging Service
Woolsey, Cheryl, 1956-
    My best friend Jesus.
    1. Children—Religious life.   2. Devotional literature—Juvenile.   3. Devotional calendars—Seventh-day Adventist.   I. Title.

242.62

ISBN 10: 0-8280-1308-X
ISBN 13: 978-0-8280-1306-6

Dedication

To Joshua, Heather, Angela, and Sarah

My Little Devotional

Contents

Key: ✎ = activity
  ✂ = craft
  ❁ = especially for toddlers

Jesus Is Born

Dear Mom and Dad
1 His Name Is Jesus ✂ ❁
2 Laid in a Manger ✎ ❁
3 Gifts for a King ✂ ❁
4 Hide and Go Seek ✎
5 A Straight Path ✎
6 Baptism ✎
7 God's Beloved Son ✂
8 God's Word ✎
9 Fishers of Men ✂
10 A Great Light ✎ ❁
11 Teacher, Preacher, Healer ✎ ❁

The Sermon on the Mount

The Beatitudes:
12 The Poor in Spirit ✂
13 The Sorrowful ✂
14 The Gentle ✂
15 People Who Love What Is Good ✂
16 The Merciful ✂
17 The Pure ✂
18 The Peacemakers ✂
19 The Persecuted ✂
20 The Salt of the Earth ✂
21 Light to the World ✂ ❁
22 Peace With Our Brother and Sister ✂
23 A Plain "Yes" or "No" ✂
24 Offer Your Left Cheek ✎
25 The Giving Heart ✎ ❁
26 The Sharing Heart ✎ ❁
27 Love Your Enemies ✂
28 Giving to Everyone ✂ ❁
29 How to Pray ✎ ❁
30 Where Is Your Treasure? ✂
31 The Lamp of the Body ✂

Contents

32 Whom Do You Serve? ✎
33 Don't Be Worried ✂ ❀
34 Look at the Lilies ✎
35 Be Careful About Judging Others ✂
36 Knock on the Door ✎ ❀
37 A Stone Instead of Bread ✎ ❀
38 The Golden Rule ✂ ❀
39 The Narrow Gate ✎
40 Good Fruit ✎ ❀
41 Real Friends ✎
42 Building on the Rock ✎ ❀
43 If You Want To ✂ ❀
44 The Soldier and the Boss ✂ ❀
45 Boss of the Wind and Sea ✂ ❀
46 The Quiet Sea ✎
47 "Your Sins Are Forgiven" ✎
48 "Follow Me" ✎
49 Eating With Sinners ✂
50 "Who Touched Me?" ✎ ❀
51 "She's Just Asleep" ✎ ❀

Symbols of Jesus
52 The Bread of Life ✂ ❀
53 The Light of the World ✎ ❀
54 Jesus Is Like a Vine ✎ ❀
55 Sun of Righteousness ✂ ❀
56 "I Am the Door" ✂ ❀
57 Living Water ✎ ❀
58 "I Am the Resurrection" ✎ ❀

The Lord's Prayer
59 "Our Father" ✂
60 "Thy Kingdom Come" ✂
61 "Our Daily Bread" ✂
62 "Forgive Us" ✂
63 "Lead Us Not Into Temptation" ✂
64 "Thine Is the Kingdom" ✂
65 Lost Sheep ✎ ❀

The Twenty-third Psalm
66 "The Lord Is My Shepherd" ✂ ❀
67 Green Pastures, Still Waters ✂ ❀
68 He Restores Us ✂ ❀

Contents

69 Paths of Righteousness ✂ ❀
70 Valley of the Shadow ✂ ❀
71 A Table Spread for Us ✂ ❀
72 My Cup, Full and Running Over ✂ ❀
73 The House of the Lord ✂ ❀
74 The Blind Men ✎ ❀
75 Grandmother's Fixed-up Back ✎ ❀
76 Perfume Bottle ✎ ❀
77 Sheep Without a Shepherd ✂
78 Give Without Charge ✎
79 Do Not Be Afraid ✎
80 When Sparrows Fall ✎
81 I Know Jesus ✎
82 Jesus' Cross ✎
83 A Cup of Cold Water ✎
84 If You Have Ears ✂
85 "Take My Yoke" ✂
86 Lord of the Sabbath ✂
87 Doing Good on the Sabbath ✂
88 God Says, "I Love You" ✂
89 A Smoldering Wick ✎
90 Jesus Saves! ✂

91 Working With Jesus ✎ ❀
92 The Holy Spirit ✂
93 Words From the Heart ✎
94 Thoughtless Words ✎
95 Greater Than Jonah and Solomon ✂
96 Jesus Is Knocking ✎
97 My Brother and Sister and Mother ✂ ❀

Jesus' Words Grow in Our Hearts

98 The Footpath ✂
99 The Rocky Soil ✂
100 Among the Thistles ✂
101 Good Soil ✂
102 The Wheat and the Weeds ✂

The Kingdom of Heaven

103 Shining Like the Sun ✂
104 The Mustard Seed ✂ ❀
105 God's Kingdom on Earth ✎
106 Yeast ✎
107 Buried Treasure ✎ ❀
108 The Best Pearl ✎

109 Honoring Our Family ✎

110 Five Loaves and Two Fish ✎ ❀

111 Jesus Makes a Miracle ✎

112 Walking on the Water ✎ ❀

113 Doing What's Important ✎

114 A Woman of Faith ✎

115 Children or Doggies? ✂

116 Signs ✎

117 The Tough Times ✂

118 Vision on the Mountain ✎

119 Faith Like a Mustard Seed ✎

120 Fishing for Money ✂

121 Who Is the Greatest? ✂ ❀

122 Angels Who Watch ✂ ❀

123 Your Brother and Sister ✎ ❀

124 Forgiving 490 Times ✎

125 Showing Mercy ✎

126 Let the Children Come ✂

127 "What Good Must I Do?" ✎

128 Following Jesus ✎

129 The Eye of a Needle ✎

130 Peter's Question ✂

131 Being Fair ✂

132 Time to Go to Jerusalem ✎

133 The Servant Leader ✂

134 The Gentle King ✎ ❀

135 A House of Prayer ✎ ❀

136 Hosanna, Again! ✎ ❀

137 The Withered Tree ✎

138 Throwing Mountains Into the Sea ✎

139 Who's Your Boss? ✂

140 The Story of Two Boys ✂ ❀

141 The Story of the Vineyard ✂

142 The Wedding Feast ✎

143 Wedding Clothes ✎

144 Caesar's Coin ✂

145 The Greatest Commandment ✂

146 The Second Commandment ✂

147 Loving Others as Yourself ✂

148 What They Say and What They Do ✎

149 Humble Yourself ✂

150 Too Bad for You ✎

151 A Clean Cup ✎ ❀

152 A Mother Hen ✎

Contents

153 Signs of Jesus' Coming ✂

154 Like Lightning ✎ ❀

155 Keep Awake! Stay Ready! ✎

156 A Story About 10 Girls ✎

157 Our Bags of Gold ✎

158 The Sheep and the Goats ✎

159 Washing Feet ✎ ❀

160 The Passover ✂

161 The Last Supper ✎ ❀

When Jesus Died for Us

162 In the Garden ✎

163 Jesus Is Betrayed ✎

164 Jesus in the Priest's Court ✂

165 Peter and the Rooster ✎

166 Judas ✎

167 Before Pilate ✎

168 "Crucify Him!" ✎

169 King of the Jews ✎

170 "Remember Me" ✎

171 Jesus' Mother ✎

172 "It Is Finished!" ✎

173 Laid in a Tomb ✎

174 Jesus Rises From the Grave ✎

175 "I Have Seen the Lord!" ✎

176 Jesus Appears to His Followers ✎

177 It Is Really Jesus! ✂

178 "My Lord and My God!" ✂

179 Breakfast on the Beach ✎ ❀

180 Coming Again ✂ ❀

List of Indexes

Index 1: Materials List

Index 2: Family or Doll Puppet Activities

Index 3: Activities and Games

Index 4: Themes

Index 5: Scripture Index

Dear Mom and Dad...

We want to make it easy for you to bring your children to Jesus every day. The short, simple devotionals in this book build on Jesus' action-based style of teaching and, generally, follow Jesus' life through the book of Matthew. The stories are short enough for you to tell in your own words, your eyes meeting your child's eyes, just as Jesus' eyes searched the hearts of His listeners.

Children (and the rest of us!) learn in many different ways. Some of us need to do things in order to learn. Some of us need to see pictures and feel objects. Some of us hear better than we see. These devotionals use a variety of learning methods to help bring a living, breathing Jesus to the fore-front of young minds and hearts in the following ways:

✂ these devotionals use plenty of hands-on activities and crafts;

✎ the activities build on the objects and events in the child's everyday life, capitalizing on Jesus' object lessons.

Please don't feel you need to follow the devotionals in order! Some you may never use; some you may use again and again. Older preschoolers will enjoy a larger variety and greater complexity. Your toddlers will like simplified versions of the devotionals that take only a few minutes and may be repeated throughout the day. We've marked those devotionals we think your very little ones will enjoy the most with a flower ❀ in the table of contents. Many children may get more out of a lesson that is *told* in the simplest terms rather than *read*. The activities you do as you explain simple stories and concepts will be the most important part of the lesson.

Lots of indexes! In the back of the book you will find helpful indexes that will be useful in individualizing your worship time specifically for your family.

Materials Index. You probably already have most of the suggested materials in your home. You may want to check over the lists, though, to prepare for upcoming lessons. If you aren't a craft person who has felt, feathers, and glitter stowed in every drawer, ask around. Most people who like to do crafts have plenty of scraps they'd be glad to share.

Family or Doll Puppet Activities Index. A number of activities suggest using family puppets or family dolls. This is a set of puppets or family dolls, one doll for each member of your family. You might want to prepare these teaching aids ahead of time. (See devotional 139 for suggestions.) Many of the small dolls, such as Barbie and Ken dolls used to reenact some of the Bible stories, can be purchased at Good Will and Salvation Army stores or other similar places. And you may also make a special box in which to keep dress-up clothes ready for these reenactments.

If your child is restless, harness that energy by choosing a devotional that includes a game from the **Activities and Games Index.**

An overview of this index will also allow you to fit certain devotionals into your monthly/yearly schedule where they will have most impact. (Are you planning a vacation at the beach? Then save devotional 179 for this time.) Much of Jesus' teaching was done outside, and with good reason! Many activities can be done outside, while on walks, or in the sandbox. Take advantage of this naturally motivating teaching arena.

Some of the activities are grouped together naturally, and build on each other. For "The Beatitudes" devotionals (12-19), you will need a scrapbook, completing a page each day. The "Symbols of Jesus" devotionals (52-58) use a basket, to which you add items every day. "The Twenty-third Psalm" devotionals (66-73) use a shoebox to create a diorama.

Some activities suggest the use of a notebook. This can be a special three-ring binder to which you can refer for these family discussions and planning activities. Sections can be created for investment plans (157), a prayer list, notes on values (113), and suggestions for improving family communication, for example.

The Themes Index is useful for those times when you need to address a particular need in your family. Perhaps a special topic will come up during the day, such as "getting along in the family" or the word "treasure" may trigger a discussion. Tie in a devotional exercise to capitalize on the interest already awakened.

And, of course, the Scripture Index, listing every Bible text used in this book, enables you to quickly locate any devotional relating to a specific passage of Scripture.

We hope you enjoy these stories, crafts, and activities as much as your little ones will. We never outgrow experience-based learning, as Jesus well knew! May He bless you and yours as you draw close to Him.

—Cheryl Lynn Woolsey

Dear Parents

His Name Is Jesus

***You are to give him the name Jesus.
Matthew 1:21, NIV.***

Materials: *old Christmas cards, markers,
yarn, hole punch.*

Craft: *card mobile.*

A long time ago an angel came down
from heaven to talk to a girl named
Mary. He said that she would have
a Baby—the most special Baby in the
world. And the angel told Mary the Baby's
name. "You are to give him the name Jesus,
because he will save his people from their
sins" (Matthew 1:21, NIV).

"Jesus" is a special name. What do you
think of when you remember Jesus? [Let each
member of the family comment.]

Let's write one letter of Jesus' name on
the back of each of these cards. [Or cut the
shape of each letter from the cards.]

We'll punch a hole in the top and bottom
of each letter, and hang them so each letter
is in order. [Hang the letters vertically.]

Now we'll hang Jesus' name where
we can see it. It will remind us to think
about Him. Now let's sing some songs
about Jesus. ●

#1

Theme: Jesus' Birth

Laid in a Manger

So she wrapped the baby with cloths and laid him in a box where animals are fed. Luke 2:7, ICV.

Materials: *small baby doll and cardboard box, or figurine of Baby Jesus and separate manger; dried grass or hay; strip of cloth for swaddling clothes.*

This Bible verse tells about what happened when Baby Jesus was first born. His mom and dad had to stay in a barn because there were no motel rooms left in the town of Bethlehem. They fixed up a manger for the new Baby to sleep in. A manger is a box that holds hay or grain for cows and other animals. It made a soft, safe, warm place for Baby Jesus to sleep.

We are going to make a bed for our doll baby Jesus to sleep in. We know that every time we do something kind for someone else, we do it for Jesus. So when you do something kind for someone, I'll give you some hay to put in the manger. When the bed is nice and soft, we'll wrap the baby in swaddling cloths and lay it in the manger.

Whom can you think of that you can help today? As you make a soft bed for Jesus, you can remember that the kind things you do are gifts for Jesus. ●

Theme: Jesus' Birth

#2

Gifts for a King

They gave him treasures of gold, frankincense, and myrrh. Matthew 2:11, ICB.

Materials: *small box, wrapping paper, bow and ribbon, scissors, tape.*

When the Wise Men came to see the baby Jesus, they brought Him presents. Do you like to give people presents? What presents do you remember giving someone? How did you feel when you gave them your present? It's a lot of fun to see the surprise and happiness in someone's face when they get a present. It makes us feel good, doesn't it?

The Wise Men brought very precious gifts to Jesus, because they knew He was a very special king. They wanted to show how glad they were that He had come to earth to help us.

When we give offerings at church, it's like the Wise Men giving their gold and expensive gifts to Jesus. It's our way of thanking Jesus for being our king, for loving us and helping us. Jesus said that when we give to others, we are giving to Him.

Let's wrap up a present for Jesus and cut a hole in the top for our money to fit through. We can put it out where we will see it every day and put our extra change in it. Then, when we find someone who needs some help, we can give it to them, or give it as an offering at church. ●

#3

Theme: Jesus' Birth ✂ ❀

Hide and Go Seek

After three days they found him. Luke 2:46, ICB.

Activity: *Hide and Go Seek.*

Every year Jesus' mom and dad went to Jerusalem. When Jesus was 12, He went with them. After the feast was over, Jesus' parents started home, but Jesus stayed behind in Jerusalem. At nightfall Jesus' mom and dad looked for Him, but He wasn't there!

Where do you think Jesus was? He was in the Temple, talking to the priests! But Jesus wasn't hiding from His mom and dad. He wouldn't make trouble for them. He had very important work to do. Remember, He was going to grow up to save His people!

When they found Jesus, they were upset. "Son," His mother asked, "why have you treated us like this?"

"Why were you searching for me?" He asked. "Didn't you know I had to be in my Father's house?" (Luke 2:48, 49, NIV).

Jesus was busy talking with the teachers in the Temple about God. What kinds of good things could *you* "get lost" doing?

Think of something good you can do, and go do it. Then I'll try to find you! ●

Theme: Service

#4

A Straight Path

"Prepare the way for the Lord. Make the road straight for him." Matthew 3:3, ICB.

Materials: *dirt, rocks, toy car.*

Jesus' cousin John was a preacher. John preached outside in the sunshine. If you went to hear John preaching, you would hear him say, "Jesus is coming! Be sorry for the things you have done wrong, and learn to do what is right." John was helping the people get ready to listen to Jesus. The Bible said John made a "straight path" for Jesus.

[Make a sandbox with rocks and dirt in a cardboard box.] Make a straight path in the dirt for this little car. Move the rocks out of the way and smooth the dirt.

We should push everything out of the way that would keep us from listening to Jesus. We turn off the TV before we have worship. We stop thinking about everything we've been doing and think about Jesus. If we've been fussing or arguing, we need to say we're sorry. Then we can feel close to everyone in our family. We'll feel close to Jesus too.

Let's pretend this rock is the television set. We'll put it out of the way. Now it's easier for us to listen to His words. What else do you want to put away so you can hear Jesus?

#5

Theme: Listening

Baptism

"I baptize you with water to show that
your hearts and lives have changed."
Matthew 3:11, ICB.

Materials: *basin of water, small doll.*

The Bible tells us about a man who helped people get ready to listen to Jesus. He was called John the Baptist because he baptized people in the Jordan River.

When people felt sorry for wrong things they'd done and wanted to live like God wanted them to, they asked John to baptize them. John would take them into the river where the water came up to their chest. They'd bend their knees a little, and John would lay them back until they were covered with water. Then he'd raise them up

like they were being raised up to live a new life as God's children.

John told them, "I baptize you with water to show that your hearts and lives have changed."

Jesus asked John to baptize Him, too. "It is right to do all that God asks us to do," Jesus said. That's why we still have baptisms. Pretend that you are John the Baptist, and you want to baptize this little doll. It wants to be part of God's family. So we'll put it under the water and raise it back up to show it wants to be God's child.

Theme: Baptism

#6

God's Beloved Son

"This is my Son and I love him. I am very pleased with him." Matthew 3:17, ICB.

Materials: *sheet of 8½" x 11" white paper, pencil.*

John the Baptist had just lifted Jesus up out of the water when two special things happened. Down through the bright sky flew a dove. This was the Spirit of God in the shape of a dove. The Holy Spirit is a person just like God and Jesus, but we can't see Him. But we know He is nearby, because we can see what He does.

When the Holy Spirit, shaped like a dove, landed on Jesus, it was a special way of honoring Him. God the Father honored Jesus too. He said, "This is my Son and I love him."

The Holy Spirit comes into our hearts like a gentle dove, helping us to love and obey God as Jesus did.

You can make a dove to remind you of the Holy Spirit. Fold this sheet of white paper in half. Place your hand on the paper, lining up your thumb along the fold. Stretch your fingers out over the paper. Keep your thumb apart from your fingers. Trace around your hand. Tear along the line you drew around your hand. When you open the shape you tore out, you should see a dove! [The thumb outlines the head; the fingers form the wings.] ●

#7

Theme: Holy Spirit

God's Word

"A person does not live only by eating bread. But a person lives by everything the Lord says." Matthew 4:4, ICB.

Materials: *basket, or large serving bowl; tea towel; Bible; songbook; Bible story books.*

fter Jesus was baptized the Holy Spirit led Him into the country. Jesus spent many days all by Himself, praying to His Father. Jesus needed His Father to help Him.

After 40 days of not eating, Jesus was hungry. Satan tried to make Him turn a stone into bread. Jesus *could* turn stone into bread if He wanted to, but He wouldn't obey Satan. Jesus told Satan, "Man does not live on bread alone, but on every word that comes from the mouth of God" (Matthew 4:4, NIV).

We all must eat in order to be healthy. Bread keeps our bodies alive. But the good things that God tells us keeps our *hearts* alive. We need to keep listening to God.

Listening to stories about Jesus, singing about Him, and praying are ways we can think about God's words.

Let's make a centerpiece for our table to show how important God's Word is. Here's a basket. We'll line it with a tea towel. What things should we put into it? [Suggest Bible, Bible story books, songbooks, etc.] ●

Theme: Listening

#8

Fishers of Men

"Come follow me. I will make you fishermen for men." Matthew 4:19, ICB.

Materials: *stiff paper, scissors, color markers, yarn.*

J esus was telling stories as He stood by a lake, talking. The people crowded closer and closer until they almost pushed Him into the water. So Jesus stepped into a fishing boat that belonged to Peter and Andrew. When He finished teaching, Jesus told Peter to go fishing.

Peter was surprised. "In the daytime? The fish are gone now!" But he dropped his net into the sea anyway. Suddenly the net was so full of fish it started to tear apart.

"Help us!" Peter called to James and John, who were in another boat. They loaded both boats so full of fish that they nearly sank.

"Come with Me," Jesus said. "From now on you will catch people."

Peter, Andrew, James, and John left their boats and went to work with Jesus.

Jesus wants everybody to be in His kingdom. And He wants His friends to help Him bring people into His kingdom. You can be a fisher for Jesus.

Let's cut out some fish and write on them the names of people we want to help know Jesus. These fish can remind you that you are fishers for Jesus. ●

Theme: Witnessing

A Great Light

"These people who live in darkness will see a great light." Matthew 4:16, ICB.

Materials: *flashlight, lamp, objects to cast shadows.*

A prophet named Isaiah wrote about what would happen when Jesus came to earth. "Now those people live in darkness. But . . . a light will shine on them" (Isaiah 9:2, ICB).

Can you think what the light was? It was Jesus! When Jesus came to teach and heal, Isaiah said, it was like a bright light shining on a dark land.

What caused the darkness that the people were living in? Old people get sick. Some people hurt each other. Jesus said that when He comes He'll do away with death. And people who listen to Jesus are always kind to each other. Jesus is the great light.

Let's make our room almost dark. We'll just leave the lamp on. Put your hand between the lamp and the wall. See the shadow. Your hand makes a dark place on the wall. But if we shine a flashlight on the dark spot it disappears. Jesus is like the light that takes away the darkness.

What things make dark shadows in your life? How can Jesus shine His light on you and take the shadows away? ●

Theme: Light

Teacher, Preacher, Healer

Jesus went everywhere in the country of Galilee. He taught in the synagogues and preached the Good News about the kingdom of heaven. And he healed all the people's diseases and sicknesses. Matthew 4:23, ICB.

Activity: *singing.*

Jesus and His friends walked all over the country of Galilee. Wherever Jesus went, crowds of people came to hear Him. He preached in the synagogues. He preached from fishing boats. He taught as He walked along the highways. And everywhere Jesus went, people brought sick friends and family to Him to be healed.

People who had headaches and people who were blind came to Jesus. Crippled people and deaf people came to Jesus. He was good news. He made everyone well.

"Did you hear what Jesus did yester-day?" moms would ask dads.

"Did you hear the stories He told today?" kids asked each other. "Come with us! We are going to see Jesus."

Maybe the children sang something like this as they went to see Jesus [sing to the tune of "Row, Row, Row Your Boat"]:

"Great news, everyone—Jesus Christ is here!
Everyone come out to see Him; Jesus Christ is here!" ●

Theme: Healing

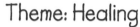

The Poor in Spirit

"Those people who know they have great spiritual needs are happy. The kingdom of heaven belongs to them." Matthew 5:3, ICB.

Materials: *blessings scrapbook, pictures of people who are experiencing a wide variety of feelings (see news magazines, children's books on feelings), paste, scissors, picture of Jesus.*

Jesus sat on a mountain with many, many people. Some didn't really care about Jesus, but many of the people sitting on the hillside felt empty in their hearts. They wanted to be close to Jesus. He filled up their empty hearts and made them feel loved and wanted. They were important to Him.

Jesus looked at these people with love, as if He were pouring all His love into their hearts. He said that those who know they need Jesus are happy. "The kingdom of heaven belongs to them." It was as though

Jesus was saying, "You may feel empty now, but all the riches of My kingdom are yours."

Do you sometimes feel as though you aren't very good or important? Tell me about it.

Let's find some pictures of people who might be feeling this way. We'll paste them in our blessings scrapbook. Write "Poor in Spirit" at the bottom of the page. Make a heart pocket to symbolize an empty heart, and put a picture of Jesus, or a paper with "Jesus Loves" written on it, in the heart to show that Jesus fills our empty heart. ●

Theme: Feelings

#12

The Sorrowful

"Those who are sad now are happy. God will comfort them." Matthew 5:4, ICB.

Materials: *blessings scrapbook, pictures of people feeling sad.*

As Jesus looked around at the people who were listening to Him on the mountain, He saw some sad faces. Can you make a sad face? What does a sad face look like? Why do you think some of these people were sad? What makes you feel sad?

Here are some pictures of people who are sad. Let's put them in our book of blessings [scrapbook].

"Blessed are the sorrowful," Jesus said. "They shall find comfort."

To be sorrowful means to be full of sorrow and sadness. Maybe you have felt sad because your puppy was lost. Maybe it made you sad to say goodbye to a friend. Jesus cares about your feelings. He knows when you are sad. You can talk to Him. He wants to help you feel better.

When we know that Jesus loves us and cares about our feelings, it's like getting a hug in our heart. Let's cut out little hearts and paste them all around our sad picture to remind us how Jesus loves us when we are sad. [Fold little squares in half, cut out half a heart, then open them.] ●

#13

Theme: Feelings

The Gentle

"Those who are humble are happy. The earth will belong to them." Matthew 5:5, ICB.

Materials: *blessings scrapbook, pictures of many kinds of people, blue and green picture or drawing of earth.*

One day some big strong soldiers came to Jesus. In those days soldiers used swords to make people obey the law. Today many soldiers use guns. Sometimes people like guns because guns help them get what they want. Sometimes even children hit others in order to get what they want. Do you know anyone like that?

Jesus loves everyone. He even loves naughty children, though He wants them to be good. It makes Him very sad when people hurt each other. Jesus said, "Blessed are the gentle; they shall have the earth for their possession" (Matthew 5:5, REB).

People who are gentle don't use force to get their own way. Gentle people use their strength to help others. They are kind and caring. Jesus will take these people to live with Him in heaven.

Let's make a page full of gentle people in our blessings scrapbook. On the opposite page we'll make a beautiful blue and green earth to show that Jesus will give the earth to kind, gentle people. ●

Theme: Feelings

#14

People Who Love What Is Good

"Those who want to do right more than anything else are happy. God will fully satisfy them." Matthew 5:6, ICB.

Materials: *blessings scrapbook; pictures of sad things such as fires or people crying; glue.*

Jesus was on a mountain when He told about the blessings. From the mountain maybe He saw a town and people hurrying back and forth. Maybe He saw farmers taking care of their crops. Everywhere people were busy. And all around Him people were sitting and listening.

"Blessed are those who want to do right more than anything else," Jesus said.

When you are very hungry and thirsty, you want to eat and drink now. You think about it all the time. Jesus said that someday children like you who really want good things to happen will be very happy. When Jesus takes us to heaven everyone will be happy. Everyone will treat each other nicely all the time.

Maybe you've seen a big kid teasing a little kid. Could you make the small child feel better? Here are some pictures that show something sad. Let's put them in our blessings scrapbook and pray that God will help us do what we can to help others.

When we want people to be kind to each other, we will be happy. ●

#15

Theme: Feelings

The Merciful

"Those who give mercy to others are happy. Mercy will be given to them."
Matthew 5:7, ICB.

Materials: *scrapbook, paper, markers, pencil, glue.*

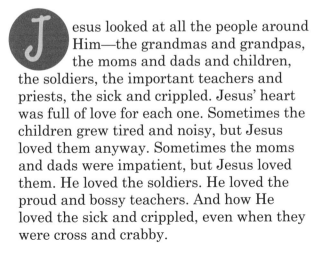esus looked at all the people around Him—the grandmas and grandpas, the moms and dads and children, the soldiers, the important teachers and priests, the sick and crippled. Jesus' heart was full of love for each one. Sometimes the children grew tired and noisy, but Jesus loved them anyway. Sometimes the moms and dads were impatient, but Jesus loved them. He loved the soldiers. He loved the proud and bossy teachers. And how He loved the sick and crippled, even when they were cross and crabby.

To be merciful means to help people, even when they don't deserve it. Jesus said, "Blessed are those who show mercy; mercy shall be shown to them" (Matthew 5:7, REB).

When we treat others kindly even though they're not too nice, we will be treated kindly too. Even when we don't deserve it.

How can you be kind to people who aren't nice to you? Jesus will fill your heart with His love and help you. Draw a picture of yourself doing something merciful and glue it in your blessings scrapbook.

Theme: Kindness

#16

The Pure

"Those who are pure in their thinking are happy. They will be with God."
Matthew 5:8, ICB.

Materials: *blessings scrapbook; dirty, white, and red hearts.*

If something is pure, it means that there's nothing in it that shouldn't be there. When you sprinkle salt on your potato, you want it to be pure—not salt that's mixed with sand!

Jesus has a special blessing for those with a pure heart. "They will see God" (Matthew 5:8, NIV). If you ask, Jesus takes away every bad thing and gives you a pure heart. One day He will take you to heaven to be with God.

Make three hearts the same size out of red, white, and dirty torn paper. Glue the dirty heart in your blessings scrapbook.

This is our heart when we hurt people by what we say and do. That's why Jesus died—to save us from all the wrong things we do. This red heart reminds us of Jesus' blood. We'll tape the top of it so it covers our dirty heart. [Face the tape so the heart can flip up to see the heart underneath.]

Now we'll put a white heart over the red. This is Jesus' pure heart. Even though we do wrong, if we ask Him Jesus puts His goodness in our lives instead of our badness! Jesus gives us His pure heart! Let's thank Him right now. [Pray with your child.] ●

Theme: Purity

The Peacemakers

"Those who work to bring peace are happy. God will call them his sons."
Matthew 5:9, ICB.

Materials: *blessings scrapbook, pieces of ribbons, picture of Jesus, tape.*

One of the blessings Jesus gave was for peacemakers. Jesus said they would be called children of God. Soldiers lived where Jesus did. It was not a peaceful time. Sometimes the people got mad at the soldiers. And the teachers and priests often argued, even in church. Mommies and daddies worried that God would never be happy with them. These people were not at peace.

Jesus wants us to have peace. He wants all children to be happy together. Peacemakers help to stop trouble. They help people learn to get along and be kind to each other. When you ask Jesus for His pure heart, He will help you be a peacemaker too.

Cut out this picture of Jesus in the shape of a circle and paste it in your blessings scrapbook. Write "peacemaker" above it. Then tape lengths of ribbon on the page. When you do something to help people get along, or help someone feel closer to Jesus, you can put one of these ribbons on your shirt. You might pin a ribbon on someone else who is being a peacemaker, too. What kinds of things can you do to be a peacemaker? ●

Theme: Peace

#18

The Persecuted

"Those who are treated badly for doing good are happy. The kingdom of heaven belongs to them." Matthew 5:10, ICB.

Materials: *blessings scrapbook; happy face stickers; pictures of Bible characters, such as Daniel, Shadrach, Meshach, and Abednego.*

Let's look through our blessings scrapbook. What kinds of people did Jesus say would have blessings? [Review.]

Jesus' last blessing was for people who have trouble because they obey God. [Older children may enjoy a quiz. Have younger children look at Bible pictures and discuss these stories and others.] Who was thrown into a lions' den because he prayed? What happened to Shadrach, Meshach, and Abednego when they wouldn't worship the golden statue?

Sometimes scary things happen to good people. But Jesus said something very surprising. If bad things happen to you when you are doing right, be happy; God will give you a rich reward in heaven.

Has anybody ever laughed at you for doing right? Maybe you were obeying your teacher or helping a child that other kids don't like. Remember what Jesus said, and be glad! [Glue pictures of persecuted Bible story characters in the blessings scrapbook. Draw happy faces around them, or use happy face stickers, and draw a picture of heaven.] ●

Theme: Feelings

The Salt of the Earth

"You are the salt of the earth. But if the salt loses its salty taste, it cannot be made salty again." Matthew 5:13, ICB.

Materials: *salt, glue, colored paper.*

Close your eyes and hold out your hand. I'm going to sprinkle something in your cupped hand. Taste it and tell me what it is. . . . It's salt!

What kind of food do you salt? Too much salt doesn't taste good, does it? But just a little helps some food taste better.

Jesus said, "You are salt to the world" (Matthew 5:13, REB). Now, why do you suppose He said that? Sometimes He said things to make us think. Jesus said that if salt didn't taste salty anymore, we would throw it away. And Jesus says we are sup-posed to be like salt!

I think He is saying that we should make a difference in people just as salt makes our food taste different. He wants you to be the kind of girl or boy that people want to have around—just as we keep the saltshaker handy on the table. Maybe He wants us to help the world taste what God's love is like. What do you think?

On a colored sheet of paper, spread some glue in the shape of a map of the earth. Now sprinkle salt on it as a reminder that we are the salt to the earth. ●

Theme: Witnessing

#20

Light to the World

"You are the light that gives light to the world. A city that is built on a hill cannot be hidden." Matthew 5:14, ICB.

Materials: *candle or lamp, matches, large metal mixing bowl. (This is a good activity for an evening devotional.)*

Let's turn out all the lights. It's hard to do anything in the dark, isn't it? [Light candle.] But now we have light. Light is important, isn't it?

Jesus said, "You are light for all the world" (Matthew 5:14, REB). One small light can be seen for a long, long way. What if I cover our light with this big mixing bowl? That would be silly, wouldn't it? What good does the light do all covered up?

Where do you think I should put the light so it would do the most good in lighting our room?

Jesus said, "Like the lamp, you must shed light among your fellows, so that, when they see the good you do, they may give praise to your Father in heaven" (verse 16, REB).

When you do the good things that Jesus wants us to do, it helps other people think about God and thank Him! When you do nice things you are spreading light! ●

#21

Theme: Witnessing

Peace With Our Brother and Sister

"If you are angry with your brother, you will be judged." Matthew 5:22, ICB.

Materials: *paper, pencil, or markers.*

Have you ever heard someone say "You're crazy"? It makes you feel bad when people talk like that, doesn't it? Jesus wants us to be very careful not to hurt each others' feelings.

"Whoever calls his brother 'good for nothing,'" Jesus said, "deserves the sentence of the court" (Matthew 5:22, REB).

Jesus is very serious about how we talk to each other. When you are playing with your brother or sister or friends, you must always be kind. When you talk to Mom and Dad, you must talk nicely.

"Make . . . peace with your brother," Jesus said (verse 24, REB).

Is there someone you need to make peace with? What can you do to get along better? Do you need to tell someone that you're sorry? Do you need to forgive someone? Do you need to be careful to say only nice things?

Draw a picture of what you want to do, or write it on a piece of paper and hang it in your room to remind you of your plan. And then do it! ●

Theme: Forgiveness

MBFJ-5

#22

A Plain "Yes" or "No"

"Say only 'yes' if you mean 'yes,' and say only 'no' if you mean 'no.'"
Matthew 5:37, ICB.

Materials: *paper, markers.*

As Jesus walked in the streets of Galilee He often heard people talking to each other. Shopkeepers and fishermen were talking. Farmers and shepherds were talking. Jesus heard the women talking as they shopped or filled their waterpots at the town well.

He loved each one of them. But He wished they could see the big world beyond their busy little world. He wanted them to understand that God was standing there listening to them and loving them. Jesus had come to the earth to show them what God is like, for Jesus *is* God.

"When you talk," He told His friends gently, "remember that you are standing in God's court. Everything around you belongs to Him. When you say things such as 'Oh, my goodness, yes,' or 'Good heavens, no,' you sound like you own these things—your goodness, your heaven. And of course, you don't own them. All these are God's!"

"[A] plain 'yes' or 'no' is all you need to say" (Matthew 5:37, REB). Make a big "NO" with your marker on one sheet of paper, and a big "YES" on another sheet of paper to help you remember Jesus' words. ●

#23

Theme: Language

Offer Your Left Cheek

"But I tell you, don't stand up against an evil person. If someone slaps you on the right cheek, then turn and let him slap the other cheek too." Matthew 5:39, ICB.

Materials: *toys.*

Has someone ever hit you, even though you weren't hurting them? Has someone grabbed something you were playing with? How do you feel when other kids aren't fair?

Maybe you get mad. You might even feel like hitting them back. And you might want to grab what's yours and just keep it.

Jesus knew that sometimes bad things happen that make us angry. Other people aren't always fair and nice, and we feel like getting even.

Jesus said, "But what I tell you is this:

Do not resist those who wrong you. If anyone slaps you on the right cheek, turn and offer him the other also" (Matthew 5:39, 40, REB).

Instead of fighting to get even, Jesus said to love those who do wrong to us.

What should you do if someone grabs your toy? Say something such as "Here, do you want this tractor, too?" [Talk about how you feel when you do this and what Jesus would do and how He would feel.] Let's ask Jesus to help us act and play the way He did. ●

Theme: Getting Along

The Giving Heart

"If a person asks you for something, then give it to him. Don't refuse to give to a person who wants to borrow from you." Matthew 5:42, ICB.

Activity: *Take a walk and talk about everything you see that is giving something away.*

Here is a poem you can sing. [It's #122 in *Happy Songs for Boys and Girls.]*

"Give," said the little stream,
"Give, oh, give; give, oh, give."
"Give," said the little stream
As it hurried down the hill.
"I am small, I know, but wherever I go,
"Give, oh, give; give, oh, give.
"I am small, I know, but wherever I go
"The fields grow greener still."
Singing, singing all the day, "Give away, give away."

Singing, singing all the day, "Give, oh, give away."
As Jesus sat on the mountain, He saw bright fields and flowers, the blue sky, and the sea of Galilee. All of nature gives to us. But Jesus, who made all things, is the biggest gift of all.

Theme: Giving

The Sharing Heart

"Give to everyone who asks you. When a person takes something that is yours, don't ask for it back." Luke 6:30, ICB.

Materials: *any two items such as toys, clothes, food, etc.*

 esus has such a giving heart. That's why He was on a mountain in Galilee, teaching the people. He came down from heaven to be with us and to help us. Everything we have, He shared with us. And He wants us to share too.

"Give to anyone who asks; and do not turn your back on anyone who wants to borrow," He says (Matthew 5:44, REB).

Sometimes it's hard to share, isn't it? When someone wants to play with your favorite toy, how do you feel? [Discuss the reasons your child might be afraid to

share—someone might break or lose a toy, etc.] Do you watch so that your friend will take good care of your toy?

[Say or sing this poem while you hold two items to share:]

"I have two dollies and I am glad.
You have no dollies and that's too bad.
I'll share my dollies 'cause I love you,
And that's what Jesus would have us do!"

Theme: Sharing

#26

Love Your Enemies

"Love your enemies. Pray for those who hurt you." Matthew 5:44, ICB.

Materials: *3" x 5" card, markers.*

Dear GOD Please love and care for Billy

o you really want to be children of God?" Jesus asked as He was teaching. What would you have said? You would have said, "Yes, I want to be God's child."

"Well," Jesus said, "God's children are different." If you are nice only to children who are nice, what is special about that? God's children will be nice to everyone.

"But I tell you, love your enemies," Jesus said. "Pray for those who hurt you" (Matthew 5:44, ICB).

Do you know someone who is unkind?

Pray for that person. Here is a prayer: Dear God, Please love and care for _____ [name]. Help [him or her] be happy and feel Your peace in [his or her] heart. Please let _____ [write down something good you want to happen to them, or something that you'd like to happen to you]. Please help me to love _____ [name] like You do. Amen.

Write this prayer on a card and decorate it. Put it beside your bed to remind yourself to pray for this person. This is a start toward turning an enemy into a friend! ●

#27

Theme: Prayer

✂

Giving to Everyone

"So you must be perfect, just as your Father in heaven is perfect."
Matthew 5:48, ICB.

Materials: *markers, white paper, small box, bow.*

Devotion

Jesus pointed to the sun. "When the sun comes up, does it shine only on the good people?" He asked. "Or does it shine on bad people, too?" Of course, it shines on good and bad people! What about the rain? Maybe He saw rain clouds over Galilee. Jesus waved His hand toward the clouds. "It rains on good people and bad people, too, doesn't it?" He said. "Your heavenly Father gives gifts of sun and rain to everyone. His goodness never stops! And that's what you should be like. There should be no limit to your goodness, either."

Do you know someone who is cranky or selfish? What kinds of gifts can you give them? What kinds of gifts can you give really nice people? [Ask children for ideas.]

Happy, encouraging words make wonderful gifts. And a smile is the most special gift of all! You can make a "smile" present to remind yourself to be happy and encouraging. Draw smiley faces of many colors on this paper. Wrap a box with your smiley wrapping paper and top it with a bow or ribbon. Put the gift box on a table to remind you to give away smiles, especially to grumpy, fussy, impatient people. ●

Theme: Giving

#28

How to Pray

"Your Father knows the things you need before you ask him." Matthew 6:8, ICB.

Activity: *song: "Whisper a Prayer."*

Jesus knew that many people wanted to talk to God but didn't know how. Some wrote prayers and waved them in the air. They thought that would make God listen. Some yelled loudly, trying to make God hear. Others tried to be extra good.

But God always listens to our prayers. Jesus felt sad that people didn't know how to pray. He had come to show them how good God was, and how to talk to Him.

Jesus said, "You don't have to be good for God to listen to you. You don't have to pray over and over either. Your Father knows what your needs are before you ask Him."

You can talk to your heavenly Father like you talk to your dad or mom. Tell Him what you are thinking, whether it is bad or good. He loves you and He already knows what you need. But He likes to hear you tell Him.

"Whisper a prayer in the morning,
Whisper a prayer at noon;
Whisper a prayer in the evening,
To keep your heart in tune."

Wherever you are, any time of the day, you can be close to God. ●

#29

Theme: Prayer

Where Is Your Treasure?

"Your heart will be where your treasure is." Matthew 6:21, ICB.

Materials: *small box, tape, metal decorative studs, brown paint.*

What are some of your special things? In Jesus' time people sometimes hid their treasure in their house or buried it out in a field. They thought that having money and treasure would save them from bad things. But who saves us from trouble? Yes! It's our Father in heaven! God gives us what we need out of His treasury in heaven!

"Don't store treasures for yourselves here on earth . . . store your treasure in heaven. The treasures in heaven cannot be destroyed by moths or rust. . . . Your heart will be where your treasure is" (Matthew 6:19, 20, ICB).

Our greatest treasure is God.

Let's make a treasure box. Cut off one side of the box's lid and tape the lid to the box. It will open and close like a treasure chest. Paint the box to look like a chest and decorate it with studs, if you like.

You can use your treasure chest to store the things we use in our worships. Your treasure chest will help you remember that our best treasure is Jesus' love for us, and our love for Him. ●

Theme: Treasure

MBFJ-6

The Lamp of the Body

"The eye is a light for the body." Matthew 6:22, ICB.

Materials: *sunglasses or colored, translucent paper, heavy paper.*

When you shut your eyes, what happens? Try it. When you open your eyes, it's like turning on the lights, isn't it? Jesus said, "The eye is a light for the body. If your eyes are good, then your whole body will be full of light" (Matthew 6:22, ICB).

What happens when you put on sunglasses? Everything looks darker, doesn't it? [Let your child look through the colored translucent paper. Point out that the color of the paper changes the color of everything you see.]

The world is filled with many beautiful things. But when some people look at the world, they don't see the nice things—only things that make them angry and unhappy. They always find something to fuss about.

But Jesus looks through eyes of love. He sees the good in people.

You can make glasses (without lenses) out of heavy paper. Pretend these are Jesus' glasses. What would you see if you were looking through Jesus' glasses? What would Jesus see if He looked around at your family? ●

#31

Theme: Light

Whom Do You Serve?

"No one can be a slave to two masters."
Matthew 6:24, ICB.

Activity: *"Mother says." [Similar to*
"Simon says."]

 et's play a funny little game. It's called "Mother says." Here goes! Mother says, "Scratch your elbow." [Child scratches elbow.]

Mother says, "Stamp your foot." [Child stamps foot. Proceed in this way for a while.]

Now we're going to have *two* masters! [Someone] will help me. [Each "master" gives a different direction at the same time. Try this several times. Discuss what happened.]

Was it hard to obey two people at the same time? When somone wants you to do one thing and you want to do another,

that's like listening to two different bosses!

Perhaps you know you ought to share, but you don't want to. It's like listening to two masters in your head: *Share toys; don't share your toys.* What do you do?

Jesus said, "No one can be a slave to two masters. . . . He will follow one master and refuse to follow the other" (Matthew 6:24, ICB). When we love God, we will love all His friends, too. And we will like to share. Which master do you want? ●

Theme: Service

#32

Don't Be Worried

"Look at the birds in the air. They don't plant or harvest or store food in barns. But your heavenly Father feeds the birds. And you know that you are worth much more than the birds." Matthew 6:26, ICB.

Materials: *whole eggshell, tacky glue, heavy paper or felt or feathers, markers.*

Talk about things that make your child afraid. Admit some of your own fears.]

The children who listened to Jesus on the mountain were afraid sometimes. Have you talked to Jesus when you were afraid? He knows all about the things that worry us, doesn't He?

Jesus knew that many of the moms and dads worried about having enough food and money. Jesus said, "Don't worry about the food you need. And don't worry about clothes. . . . Look at the birds in the air.

They don't plant or harvest or store food in barns. But your heavenly Father feeds the birds. . . . You are worth much more than the birds" (Matthew 6:25, 26, ICB).

Let's make a bird finger puppet from this egg. Use a needle to poke holes at both ends of the shell. Blow out the egg white and yolk, and wash and dry your eggshell. Glue a beak to the front and tail feathers to the back and decorate your bird with markers. Glue the end of a short roll of paper to the bottom of the bird. It will remind you of God's love! ●

Theme: Worry

Look at the Lilies

*"And why do you worry about clothes?
Look at the flowers in the field."
Matthew 6:28, ICB.*

Materials: *real flowers (preferably wild).*

Jesus said something that must have made the kids sitting around Him laugh: "Look at the lilies out in the fields. Are they out there working hard, trying to make money to buy clothes? Do they have sewing machines so they can make their own clothes? No! God makes the clothes for these lilies. Even the richest, wisest king there ever was, King Solomon, didn't have clothes as nice as these little flowers!

"Now, if God takes all this trouble to dress these beautiful flowers, which are here today and gone tomorrow, don't you think He will dress you?"

"Don't have so little faith! Don't worry and say, . . . 'What will we wear?' Your Father in heaven knows what you need. The thing you should want most is God's kingdom and doing what God wants. Then all these other things you need will be given to you. So don't worry about tomorrow" (Matthew 6:30-34, ICB).

You don't have to be afraid of a single thing! Your heavenly Father knows about everything you need. Let's find some flowers that God has dressed up and make a bouquet for our table. ●

Theme: Worry

#34

Be Careful About Judging Others

"Don't judge other people, and you will not be judged." Matthew 7:1, ICB.

Material: *wood scrap (1" x 4").*

Often Jesus said things in a funny way so that people wouldn't forget His lessons. Once He talked about people walking around with big boards in their eyes.

Have you ever had dirt in your eyes? It really hurts, doesn't it? Jesus told the people, "Why do you say to your brother, 'Let me take that little piece of dust out of your eye'? Look at yourself first! You still have that big piece of wood in your own eye" (Matthew 7:4, 5, ICB).

This was Jesus' way of saying "How can you fuss about all the little faults other people have and not even notice the great big faults you have? Straighten out yourself before you try to straighten out someone else." Tattletales say, "Mom, brother is being bad," or "Dad, sister lost your screwdriver." When I was a tattletale, my mom or dad would say, "You need to pay attention to number one." They wanted me to make sure that I was doing what was right and not worry about what my sisters were doing.

If you want to remember not to be a tattletale, write a big figure "1" on a piece of board to remind you about Jesus' lesson.

Theme: Judging

Knock on the Door

"Continue to knock, and the door will open for you." Matthew 7:7, ICB.

Materials: *a quarter or other small gift for each child, five spoons, a door. Before worship, hide the spoons.*

I have something for you. If you ask me, I'll give it to you. [Hand out a small gift as each child asks for it.] There are five spoons in our room. See if you can find them all. [Allow time to find spoons.] How did I know spoons were in here? Yes! I put them there.

Now I'm going to stand behind this door. When you knock, I'll open it, OK? [Try this with the child several times if he or she enjoys it.] How did you know I'd open the door? I said I would, didn't I?

Let's sit down and I'll read something

Jesus said. He said, "Continue to ask, and God will give to you. Continue to search, and you will find. Continue to knock, and the door will open for you. Yes, everyone who continues asking will receive" (Matthew 7:7, 8, ICB).

[Discuss parallels between your games and these verses.] I wanted you to ask me for something special because I had something special for you! In the same way, Jesus wants us to ask because He has things to give us! What special things do we really need that Jesus wants to give us? ●

Theme: Prayer

#36

A Stone Instead of Bread

"What would you do if your son asks for bread?" Matthew 7:9, ICB.

Materials: *parent dolls (such as Barbie and Ken) and a child doll (sized proportionately to parent dolls), or pictures of parents and a child cut from magazines or catalog.*

Use the dolls or cutouts to tell the following story.]

Here's Mom, and here's Dad. And this is _____ [your child's name]. One day _____ [child] came to Mom and Dad. "I'm hungry," _____ [child] said. "May I have an apple?"

"Yes, here is a big red apple," Mom said.

Then _____ [child] went to Dad. "Dad," _____ [child] said, "I'm so hungry! Please give me a piece of bread."

So Dad cut _____ [child] a thick slice of bread from the loaf Mom had made.

It makes Mom and Dad happy to give good things to you because you are our special child. Jesus told moms and dads, "Even though you're not as loving as God is, you know how to give good gifts to your children. So surely your heavenly Father will give good things to those who ask him" (Matthew 7:11, ICB).

Jesus loves you even more than Mom and Dad do! He loves to give you good things when you ask. ●

#37

Theme: Giving

The Golden Rule

"Do for other people the same things you want them to do for you."
Matthew 7:12, ICB.

Materials: *gold stars (or a yellow marker), doll figures to act out scenarios.*

ave you ever heard of the golden rule? Here it is: "Do for other people the same things you want them to do for you." Let's act out some stories and learn the golden rule.

Here's a little girl who just fell down. She's crying and holding her knee. If you fell down and were hurt, what would you want someone to do for you? [Discuss.]

Let's pretend this other little doll is you. How can you help this little girl who fell?

Here's another story. This little boy is new here, and he doesn't have any friends yet.

How would you feel if you didn't have any friends? What would you want someone to do for you? OK, here you are again [show doll]. What can you do to help this lonely boy?

[Another scenario to try:] Mom is tired, Sister spilled her milk, and the table is covered with supper dishes. Dad is in a hurry and can't find his keys. If you were Mom or Dad, how would you feel? What would you like someone to do for you? The golden rule.

We'll write this special rule on a card and put gold stars around it [or color it yellow]. ●

Theme: Kindness

#38

The Narrow Gate

"Enter through the narrow gate."
Matthew 7:13, ICB.

Materials: *blocks, cars, toy people. Let child build wall with gate opening.*

Let's build a wall that has two gates. One gate is very wide, and a wide road leads up to it. [Build wall.] This gate is so wide that two or three toy cars can go through it at once!

Now let's make a gate in the wall that is so narrow only one person can get through.

Jesus told a story about two gates. "The road that leads to [destruction] is a very easy road. And the gate . . . is very wide. . . . But the gate that opens the way to true life is very small. . . . Only a few people find that road" (Matthew 7:13, 14, ICB).

Lots of people go through the wide gate, but that way does not go to heaven. That is not the way to go to live with God.

If we want to live forever with Him, Jesus said we should go through the narrow gate. But many people don't want to do things God's way. They don't even think about looking for His gate.

Let's ask God, "What's Your way?" It isn't hard to find the narrow gate when we ask God. And when we find it, we start to really live! That's the beginning of heaven. ●

#39

Theme: Choosing

Good Fruit

"You will know these people because of the things they do." Matthew 7:16, ICB.

Materials: *pictures of fruit trees or a vegetable garden or a real orchard or garden, and real fruit and vegetables.*

M ake a matching game: Draw, or cut out, pictures of fruits or vegetables. Create matching pairs—an apple and an apple tree, a tomato and tomato plant, etc. Ask the child to match each fruit or vegetable to the plant it comes from.]

How did you know where the fruits and vegetables grew? Did you see other apples on the apple tree? That's one good way to recognize an apple tree, isn't it? But there aren't always apples on apple trees. In the winter the tree doesn't even have any leaves. In the spring it has flowers before

the apples start growing. When fall comes, the apples are ready to be picked.

Jesus asked the people a question: "Do people pick grapes from thorn bushes, or figs from thistles?" (Matthew 7:16, NIV). Even the children listening knew that answer!

"No, of course not!" they said, laughing.

You'll be able to tell children who love Jesus by the good things they do. Jesus says, "By their fruit you will recognize them" (verse 16, NIV). What kinds of nice things do you want to do? ●

Theme: Obedience

#40

D e v o t i o n

Real Friends

"The only people who will enter the kingdom of heaven are those who do the things that my Father in heaven wants." Matthew 7:21, ICB.

Materials: *a sign that reads "Heaven."*

Once Jesus said something that made the kids who were listening stop and think. He talked about people who thought they loved Jesus, but they didn't. Let's pretend it's time to go to heaven! [Put "heaven" sign on door.] I'll pretend to be Jesus. [Coach an adult or older child to be rejected person who tells all the "good" things he/she has done. Use Bible as basis. You answer, "I never knew you," and shut the door.]

Why will this sad thing happen? Jesus said: "The only people who will enter the kingdom of heaven are those who do the things that my Father in heaven wants" (Matthew 7:21, ICB). What kinds of things does God want? [Kindness; helping, etc.] Jesus wants us to be real friends with Him. What do real friends do? [Discuss: we really listen, we care about what our friends like, we do what makes them happy.]

Let's try that scene at heaven's door again. [This time, when child knocks, welcome him or her, emphasizing, "I've known you a long time. We are good friends because we really care about each other. I'm so glad you've come to live with Me!"] ●

#41

Theme: Friendship

Building on the Rock

"The wise man built his house on rock."
Matthew 7:24, ICB.

Materials: *sand in large tub or sandbox,*
cardboard box or blocks, water.

et's sing the song "The Wise Man
Built His House Upon a Rock."
[Use actions.]
Jesus told the story about the wise man
and the foolish man. Let's read it. "The wise
man built his house on rock. It rained hard
and the water rose. The winds blew and hit
that house. But the house did not fall. . . .
But the person who hears the things I teach
and does not obey them is like a . . . foolish
man [who] built his house on sand. It
rained hard, the water rose, and the winds
blew and hit that house. And the house fell

with a big crash" (Matthew 7:24-27, ICB).
Let's see what happens if we build on
sand. [Make a little house out of blocks,
cardboard, etc.] When it rains hard and the
flood come up, what happens to the sand
our house is built on? [Spray water from
hose, or use cups of water, to wash away
sand.] Sand washes quickly away, and our
house has nothing to stand on.

But when we do what Jesus says, it's like
building on rock. We will always know what
is right, even though all kinds of storms push
us around. Jesus' words make us strong. ●

Theme: Listening

#42

If You Want To

"Lord, you have the power to heal me if you want." Jesus touched the man and said, "I want to heal you. Be healed!" Matthew 8:2, 3, ICB.

Materials: *paper, markers.*

Moms and dads and children followed Jesus down the mountain. They still wanted to be nearby. Then a poor sick man came to Jesus. He had leprosy, and people were very afraid of him. They thought he would make them sick too. People with leprosy had to live far away from the towns. They had to call out, "Unclean, unclean!" so people would know to stay away.

But this dirty, sick leper came to Jesus. The people screamed and ran away. But Jesus didn't. Jesus loved him just the way he was.

The leper bowed. "'Sir, if only you will, you can make me clean.' Jesus stretched out his hand and touched him, saying, 'I will; be clean'" (Matthew 8:2, 3, REB). And the sick man was well!

Jesus wants to help us out of our troubles too. Let's make cutouts of hands to put up on your wall. Trace a big hand [adult] reaching down. Trace your hand reaching up. Cut them out and tape them on your wall. They will remind you that Jesus always wants to reach out to help you. ●

Theme: Salvation

The Soldier and the Boss

"All you need to do is command that my servant be healed, and he will be healed." Matthew 8:8, ICB.

Materials: *picture of Jesus, yarn, paper, markers. Explain definition of "centurion": a soldier who is boss over 100 soldiers.*

One day a centurion came to ask Jesus' help. "Lord, my servant is at home in bed. He . . . is in much pain" (Matthew 8:6, ICB).

Jesus said that He would come, but the centurion said No. "You're the boss over everything," he said. "I'm a boss over 100 soldiers, and they do what I tell them to do. But You're a bigger boss. If You say my servant will get well, he will."

Jesus was surprised. Hardly anybody believed He was that big a boss. A boss over *everything?* Everywhere?

This soldier believed that whatever Jesus said would happen—here in front of Him, or away in someone's house. He knew that Jesus was really and truly the boss of everything!

Jesus said to the centurion, "'Go home. Your servant will be healed just as you believed he would.' And at that same time his servant was healed" (verse 13, ICB).

[Have each person in the family draw a picture of something Jesus is in charge of—sickness, politics, our hearts, etc. Write "The Boss" under a picture of Jesus. Use the yarn to make lines from Jesus to pictures.] ●

Theme: Faith

#44

Boss of the Wind and the Sea

"Then Jesus got up and gave a command to the wind and the sea." Matthew 8:26, first part, ICB.

Materials: *paper, markers.*

Jesus was very tired. All day He had taught the people and healed the sick. Everyone needed something. They all crowded close, jostling Him. Jesus knew He needed to rest.

So Jesus got into a nearby boat and lay down. It was so peaceful and quiet riding on the water that He fell fast asleep.

Suddenly a big storm blew up. The waves tossed the boat up and down. The wind shrieked across the sea, slashing off tops of waves and filling the boat with water. Jesus' friends, who were trying to row the boat, were terrified. They had been out in lots of storms, but none so bad as this one.

Still, Jesus slept on and on. He wasn't worried at all. The howling wind didn't wake Him up. His friends shook Him awake. "'Lord, save us!' they cried. 'We will drown!'"

"Jesus answered, 'Why are you afraid? You don't have enough faith.' Then Jesus . . . told the wind . . . to be still. The wind stopped, and the sea became very calm" (Matthew 8:25, 26, ICB).

Draw pictures of storms to add to your collection of what Jesus is boss over. ●

#45

Theme: Trust

The Quiet Sea

"The wind stopped and the sea became very calm." Matthew 8:26, last part, ICB.

Activity: *Use poem as a finger play or use props such as a coat, a board, and a baby doll to act out poem.*

J esus climbed one night into a little
      fishing boat,
   And wrapped Himself up in a fish-
erman's coat,
He lay down to rest on a rough wooden board
And went right to sleep, not saying a word.
Rock, rock, rock, rock. [gently]

The wind swept down and ripped at the sails,
The waves tossed high and frothed in
    the gale,
But Jesus slept on in the wild, wet weather
Like a baby asleep in the arms of its mother.

Rock, rock, rock, rock! [wildly]

"Wake up, dear Lord! Lord, save us!"
   we cried.
"We're sinking! We'll drown and be lost in
   the tide!"
"Be still!" He commanded, and the wind
   did no harm.
Rock, rock, rock, rock. [gently]

Theme: Trust

#46

"Your Sins Are Forgiven"

"But I will prove to you that the Son of Man has authority on earth to forgive sins." Luke 5:24, ICB.

Materials: *Ken doll, blocks, small cardboard bed, string.*

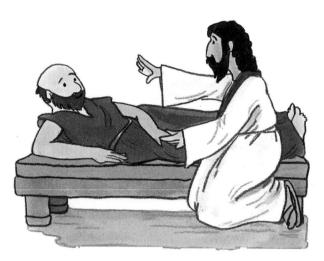

So many people crowded around Jesus that sometimes sick people had a hard time getting close. One man was so anxious to see Jesus that his friends carried him on his bed up to the roof of the house where Jesus was teaching. They made a hole in the roof and let the man down through the hole to Jesus.

"Jesus . . . said to the sick man, 'Friend, your sins are forgiven'" (Luke 5:20, ICB).

The people crowding the room started talking. "Who is this man? . . . Only God can forgive sins" (verse 21, ICB).

"Jesus knew what they were thinking. He said . . . 'Which is easier: to tell this paralyzed man, "Your sins are forgiven," or to tell him, "Stand up and walk"'?" (verses 22, 23, ICB). "So Jesus said . . . 'I tell you, stand up! Take your mat and go home.'" (verse 24, ICB). The man jumped up, picked up his mat, and hurried home, praising God.

[Use props to act out this story. Discuss how we feel when Jesus forgives.] We feel like this man who jumped up from his bed, praising God. Jesus frees us from doing bad things. ●

#47

Theme: Forgiveness

"Follow Me"

When Jesus was leaving, he saw a man named Matthew. Matthew was sitting in the tax office. Jesus said to him, "Follow me." And Matthew stood up and followed Jesus. Matthew 9:9, ICB.

Activity: *role play.*

From the first time Matthew saw Jesus, he helped Him with His work of helping the people. He listened to Jesus' lessons. What was important to Jesus was important to Matthew, too.

Let's imagine that today Jesus walked up _____ [your street] and knocked on _____ [number of your house]. Dad is busy. Mom is busy. _____ [your child's name] is busy. Jesus looks at us and says, "Follow me!"

[Discuss this step. Do we want to follow Jesus? How can you follow Jesus today?]

Dad gets up and goes with Jesus. Mom gets up and goes with Jesus. _____ [child] gets up and goes with Jesus. We can follow Jesus even though we can't see Him. What would Jesus do if He were here today? Let's pretend He's here. Now, what would He do? What would we do?

How can we help Him today? ●

Theme: Obedience

#148

Eating With Sinners

"I did not come to invite good people. I came to invite sinners." Matthew 9:13, ICB.

Materials: *two colors of paper, pencils.*

J esus loved people and they loved Him too. All kinds of people invited Jesus to visit them: cheaters, drunkards, lazy people. Often teachers and the priests stayed away from sinners. They wanted everyone to think they were good. They were afraid of looking bad.

"Why does Jesus eat with all these bad people?" they asked.

Jesus answered them. "It is not the healthy who need a doctor, but the sick" (Matthew 9:12, NIV).

Jesus had come to help people with prob-

lems. Some people didn't think they needed any help. So Jesus went to eat with the people who knew they needed Him. He listened to them as they told Him about their troubles, and was their friend.

[Set a place at your table for Jesus. Give everyone two pieces of colored paper. On one paper, write some good news to tell Jesus. On the other, write about a problem you want Jesus to help you with. You can help your child write or draw his/her contributions. As you say grace, share each message to Jesus, then lay each paper on Jesus' plate.] ●

#49

Theme: Hospitality

"Who Touched Me?"

"Be happy, dear woman. You are made well because you believed." Matthew 9:22, ICB.

Materials: *robes and headpieces for actors. The more members of your family who act in the story the better!*

A man named Jairus came to see Jesus. He was very worried. "My daughter is dying. Please come and touch her, and she will live," he pleaded.

Jesus got up to go with Jairus. But crowds of people pressed so close to Jesus that He could hardly breathe. Suddenly Jesus stopped. "Who touched Me?" He asked.

Peter exclaimed, "All these people are touching You all the time!"

"Someone touched Me," Jesus insisted. "I felt power go out from Me."

A woman came and fell at His feet. "I just touched the bottom of Your robe," she said, trembling. "For years and years doctors tried to make me well, but no one could help me. But You made me well when I touched Your robe!"

"Daughter, your faith has healed you," Jesus said, "Go in peace."

Jesus knows when you need Him, no matter how many others need Him too.

[Have each person in your family pick a character in this story, and act it out.]

But our story isn't finished. We'll finish the story of Jairus' daughter tomorrow. ●

Theme: Healing

#50

"She's Just Asleep"

"The girl is not dead. She is only asleep."
Matthew 9:24, ICB.

Materials: *robes and head coverings to act out story.*

The lady who had touched Jesus' robe was just thanking Him for healing her when someone pushed through the crowd to speak to Jairus. "Your daughter just died," he said, all out of breath. "Don't trouble Jesus anymore."

"Don't worry," Jesus told Jairus. "Have faith, and she will be well." When they came to Jairus' house, everyone was weeping. "Stop crying," Jesus said. "She isn't dead. She's only sleeping." Jesus sent everyone out of her room except Peter, James, John, and the girl's parents. Jesus took the girl's hand and called, "Get up, little girl!" She opened her eyes and sat up!

"Give her something to eat," Jesus told her mom. So Mom hurried to find something special for her little girl to eat.

Why did Jesus say the little girl was sleeping? [Discuss.] Maybe Jesus wanted to remind us that He made us. For Him, death is just a sleep till He wakes us up when He comes.

[Act out story, including disciples and mourners. Act out yesterday's and today's lessons together.] ●

#51

Theme: Death

The Bread of Life

"I am the bread that gives life."
John 6:35, ICB.

Materials: *ingredients for making bread or a slice of bread, ribbon or thread. Make a hole in a slice of bread, through which you tie one end of a ribbon or thread. Let it dry for a day.*

The next seven devotionals are about symbols Jesus used. Add each item to a large basket as you complete each devotional, reviewing the symbols often. You might add other symbols later as you and your child discover them.]

When Jesus lived on this earth, He ate bread almost every day. Do you eat bread every day? Some people eat tortillas every day; others eat rice or potatoes or corn for the main part of their meal. When Jesus told the people He was the Bread of Life, He wanted them to think about how much they needed bread. It was their main food. Jesus wanted the people to think of Him when they ate their food.

"Listening to My stories and lessons is like eating good bread," He said. "My stories and lessons help you grow up strong and healthy, just as bread does. You need to listen to My words every day."

We'll let this piece of bread remind us that Jesus said He is the Bread of life. ●

Theme: Bread

#52

The Light of the World

"I am the light of the world. The person who follows me will never live in darkness." John 8:12, ICB.

Materials: *lightbulb or candle, blindfold.*

Jesus stood on the steps of the Temple. It was festival time, and bright festival lights surrounded Him. The Temple was a place to come and worship God, to think about Him, and to thank Him for His goodness.

Now Jesus stood before all the people. He was God, as well as a human being, and He cried aloud to all the people who had come to worship. "I am the light of the world. No follower of mine shall walk in darkness; he shall have the light of life" (John 8:12, REB).

Shut your eyes and see if you can walk about the room. [Use a blindfold if the child desires one.]

Without light, our world would be as dark as if we were blind. Jesus is our light. When we look at Him and listen to His words, we know where to go and what to do so we don't stumble and fall as we would if we were walking in darkness. Jesus shows us what is good and right.

Let's put a lightbulb (or candle) in our basket to remind us that Jesus is our light. ●

#53

Theme: Light

Jesus Is Like a Vine

"I am the vine, and you are the branches." John 15:5, ICB.

Materials: *grapevine, or other vine.*

Grapevines were planted in rows beside the road where Jesus and His friends were walking. Stakes and rope, stretched across the rows, held the vines off the ground so the grapes would not be crushed on the ground.

Jesus said to His friends, "Imagine Me as a true, strong vine growing up from the ground. You are like My branches." What happens if a branch gets broken off from the vine? It can't grow anymore. It can't grow grapes. It isn't connected to the life-giving vine, and it dies.

If we stay close to Jesus, His words in our hearts give us life. Just like the juices from the vine give life to the branch. We can grow good fruit—peace and joy and happiness—and we will love to be kind to others. Without Jesus, we can't have any of these fruits. I want to stay close to Jesus, don't you? I want His words to live in my heart so I will have lots of His fruit.

Put a piece of grapevine into the basket as a reminder that Jesus is the true vine. ●

Theme: Growing

#54

MBFJ-9

Sun of Righteousness

"Goodness will shine on you like the sun."
Malachi 4:2, ICB.

Materials: *yellow, orange, red tissue paper;*
glue; Styrofoam ball.

Malachi wrote about Jesus' coming. Malachi said that for those who honor God's name, "the sun of righteousness will rise with healing in its wings, and you will break loose like calves released from the stall" (Malachi 4:2, REB).

Malachi makes a word picture to help us imagine what Jesus is like. Think of how long winter must seem to a calf penned up in a barn. Then spring comes and the world gets warm, and new green grass grows. The calves are freed to run out into the warm sunshine.

Pretend you are a calf, rushing out into the sunshine. How would it feel to be free to run and jump and play? Show me what you would do! [Let child play like a calf.]

Jesus brings us light and life and healing. With Jesus in our lives, we feel as free and happy as calves playing in the sun!

Wad newspaper into a ball and wrap it with yarn, or use a Styrofoam ball. Glue tissue paper to the ball. Put this "sun" in your basket to remind you that Jesus is like a sun of righteousness, rising with healing in its wings. ●

Theme: Jesus is like . . .

"I Am the Door"

"I tell you the truth. I am the door for the sheep." John 10:7, ICB.

Materials: *heavy paper, Jesus' face sticker.*

Jesus told a story about a shepherd taking his sheep into a sheepfold, a fenced-in place, where they will be safe at night. In the morning the shepherd opens the door. He calls his sheep by their names. They recognize his voice and come running. There is only one door to the sheepfold. Anyone who sneaks over the wall instead of using the door is a robber!

Jesus told the people a word picture to show them what He was like. "I am the door of the sheepfold. . . . Anyone who comes into the fold through me will be safe. He will go in and out and find pasture" (John 10:7-9, REB).

When we do things the way Jesus tells us to, we will be safe and happy. But sometimes people try to tell us, "You don't need to listen to Jesus. There are other ways of living a good life." These people are robbers, Jesus says. You will not be safe following them. "I am the only right door to a good life."

Cut a door in a heavy piece of paper or cardboard. Put a sticker of Jesus' face on the door. Put the cardboard with the door cut in it into your basket of symbols of Jesus. ●

Theme: Salvation

#56

Living Water

"The water I give will become a spring of water flowing inside him." John 4:14, ICB.

Materials: *bottled spring water.*

Remember how Jesus said that people who came to Him for the bread of life would never be hungry? Then He added, "Whoever believes in me will never be thirsty" (John 6:35, REB).

"The water that I shall give will be a spring of water within him, welling up and bringing eternal life" (John 4:14, REB).

The water in this bottle comes from a spring. Water in a spring never stops flowing. It keeps pouring out of the ground. Spring water is tasty and fresh and pure. That's why we like to drink it.

The water Jesus promises us is free. His words in our hearts are like a spring of water. They keep bringing more and more happiness. They never stop giving us life. Isn't that a beautiful word picture of Jesus?

[If you know of a spring nearby, go to visit it and think of Jesus giving us happiness like a spring of running water.]

You can put the bottled spring water in the basket to remind us of Jesus' living water. ●

57

Theme: Salvation

"I Am the Resurrection"

"I am the resurrection and the life. He who believes in me will have life even if he dies." John 11:25, ICB.

Activity: *Place something living (such as a plant) in the basket to represent life.*

Jesus' good friend Lazarus had died. Mary and Martha loved Jesus, but they were sad Jesus hadn't come in time to heal their brother, Lazarus.

"Lazarus will rise again," Jesus promised.

"I know he will rise at the resurrection," Martha answered.

Jesus told her, "I am the resurrection and the life. Whoever has faith in me shall live, even though he dies" (John 11:25, REB).

Then Jesus went to the tomb and called Lazarus. Lazarus had been dead four days. But he heard Jesus' call and awoke from the dead. If Jesus' words brought a dead man to life, what do you think they can do for you? Jesus created the world by the breath of His mouth. His call raises the dead. Everything He does and says is life to us!

What would you like to put into our basket to show that Jesus is life? You can draw a picture of someone coming out of the grave. Or you might use something that has life in it, like a plant, to show that Jesus is life. ●

Theme: Death

#58

"Our Father"

"Our Father in heaven, we pray that your name will always be kept holy." Matthew 6:9, ICB.

Materials: *4" x 6" cards or poster board, markers, glitter, glue, sponge.*

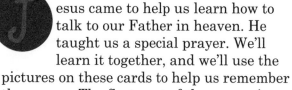esus came to help us learn how to talk to our Father in heaven. He taught us a special prayer. We'll learn it together, and we'll use the pictures on these cards to help us remember the prayer. The first part of the prayer is this: "Our Father in heaven, hallowed be your name" (Matthew 6:9, NIV).

God, our Father, lives in heaven. Soon Jesus is coming to take us to heaven. It will be very exciting when we see Jesus and our Father for the very first time!

Our Father's name is very holy. It is a very sacred, special name, because God, our Father, is perfect and wonderful and strong. That is why we treat His name very carefully. We don't say "Jesus" or "God" except when we are talking very respectfully about them.

Write "Our Father" in beautiful letters on a card. Draw a cloud around the letters to show heaven. Cut out the cloud and glue it on top of another card with some little blocks of sponge or paper under the cloud so it will stick up, away from the bottom card. ●

Theme: Prayer (God's name)

"Thy Kingdom Come"

"We pray that your kingdom will come."
Matthew 6:10, ICB.

Materials: *4" x 6" cards, (picture of New Jerusalem, optional).*

The next part of the prayer Jesus taught says "Your kingdom come, your will be done on earth as it is in heaven" (Matthew 6:10, NIV). Jesus told lots of stories of what the kingdom of heaven is like. God the Father is king there. The rules in the kingdom are fair and they help people stay happy. Our Father loves everyone in His kingdom, and they all love Him back. All are kind to each other. When we do our Father's will, we do what He wants us to do. That makes Him the king of our lives, and we will be happy.

Many here on earth want to be their own king. They aren't good kings, so we have lots of trouble with them. Jesus told us to pray and ask our Father to bring His wonderful kingdom here, to our earth, so we can be happy like the angels in heaven.

On the right side of your card, draw a world with hearts around it. On the left side put a picture of the New Jerusalem, with a red arrow pointing toward the earth and our hearts. That shows that we want our Father to bring His kingdom to this earth and to be the king of the whole world. ●

Theme: Prayer (heaven)

#60

"Our Daily Bread"

"Give us the food we need for each day."
Matthew 6:11, ICB.

Materials: *4" x 6" card, picture or drawing of bread.*

Do you remember the first two parts of the Lord's Prayer we have learned? [Review cards.] The next part of the Lord's Prayer asks our Father to take care of us. "Give us today our daily bread" (Matthew 6:11, NIV).

Every day our Father gives us many things. We breathe air in and out all day long. Can you think of other things we use every day? [Discuss such things as water, food, clothes, love, a warm, safe place to live.]

"Daily" means every day. Every day, Jesus went to His Father and asked Him for the things He needed that day. He wants us to do that too. We don't have to worry about anything. All we need to ask for is what we need today. Our Father loves us so much that day after day He gives us these things.

On our card, let's put a picture of bread to remind us of this part of the Lord's Prayer. If you like to draw, try drawing a pair of hands holding the bread. ●

#61

Theme: Prayer (God's Care)

"Forgive Us"

"Forgive the sins we have done."
Matthew 6:12, ICB.

Materials: *4" x 6" cards, red paper or*
heart stickers.

L et's say the first parts of the Lord's Prayer together. [Review with cards.] The next part asks our Father to forgive us. "Forgive us our debts, as we also have forgiven our debtors" (Matthew 6:12, NIV). We are asking God to forgive us for the things we should have done, but didn't—or the things we shouldn't have done, but we did.

When the Father forgives us, He acts as though He has forgotten that we ever did anything bad, and treats us as though we have always been good. Isn't that a wonder-ful thing for Him to do?

But if we ask the Father to forgive us, we should forgive people who do us wrong. It's as if the Father is saying, "If I forget the wrong things you did, you should forget the wrong things other people do to you, and love them just as I love you."

On our card let's write some of the things we have done wrong. Then we'll ask our Father to forgive us. We'll cover the bad things we did with big red hearts or stickers to show that our Father wipes out all the bad things we did and loves us anyway. ●

Theme: Prayer (forgiveness)

MBFJ-10

#62

"Lead Us Not Into Temptation"

"Do not cause us to be tested."
Matthew 6:13, ICB.

Materials: *4" x 6" cards (dirty or messy), markers, small photo of child, yellow or gold paper, scissors.*

The part of the Lord's Prayer we'll learn today says "And lead us not into temptation, but deliver us from the evil one" (Matthew 6:13, NIV).

A temptation is something that makes us want to do something we shouldn't do. If you see a toy that belongs to someone else and you want it, you are tempted to take it. What else could be a temptation to you? Jesus told us to ask God to help us not do the things we shouldn't. If we ask Him, God the Father will help us do what is right.

The Father will help us when sad and bad things happen. Since the Father isn't king in everyone's heart, some people still do bad things. But God will always be near us, and help us when these things happen. He will keep us from danger and from people who do wrong.

This messy card stands for bad things that happen. Here is a picture of us [place picture of child in center of card] right in the middle of trouble. Draw a golden ray of light from the top of the card all around us. This reminds us of God's help, saving us from bad things. ●

63

Theme: Prayer (temptation)

"Thine Is the Kingdom"

"For thine is the kingdom, and the power, and the glory, for ever. Amen."
Matthew 6:13.

Materials: *4" x 6" cards, markers, glitter, glue.*

N ow we'll learn the last part of the Lord's Prayer: "For thine is the kingdom, and the power, and the glory, for ever. Amen." This means that our Father is the king of the universe, and the king of our hearts. We tell God, "We give You glory by obeying You and showing that people who live in Your care are happy and peaceful. You are the most powerful one in the whole universe, but You love each one of us as though there were no others to love and care for. You have always been, and always will be, king of everything."

Angels love to worship our Father. His goodness makes them want to sing. So we end our prayer praise just as the angels love to praise God. Let's imagine we're with the angels, singing to God. When Jesus comes, He'll take us to heaven so we can see God's loving face.

Won't that be fun! But we don't have to wait to sing to the Father. Let's sing right now! [Let child choose song.] On your last card draw a picture of an angel standing beside us as we sing to the Father. [Or glue a picture of an angel and your child on card.] •

Theme: Prayer (praise)

#64

Lost Sheep

"Be happy with me because I found my lost sheep." Luke 15:6, ICB.

Materials: *100 large beans for sheep, rocks for a sheepfold, small stick for shepherd, other sticks for friends.*

elp your child count out 100 beans. Using rocks, make a sheepfold.]

Jesus told a story about a shepherd who had 100 sheep. The shepherd loved each one. Every night he counted them to make sure they were all safely home. But one night, one sheep was missing. [Have child "hide" one bean, then count "sheep" again.] There were only 99 sheep! The shepherd could have said, "Oh, well, I still have lots of sheep. It's too dark and cold to hunt for one little sheep."

But he didn't say that. He thought of how cold and frightened his lost sheep was feeling. He hurried out into the dark night and looked and looked until he finally found it. [Let the "shepherd" stick find the lost "sheep."]

The sheep was scared and cold, so the shepherd put it on his shoulders and brought it safely home. Then he called all his friends together, and they had a big party to celebrate. Jesus loves us just as the shepherd loved that sheep. He will go out in the worst storm to find just one person who feels lost and far away from Him. He is our good shepherd. ●

#05

Theme: Jesus' Love

"The Lord Is My Shepherd"

I have everything I need. Psalm 23:1, ICB.

Materials: *cardboard shoe box; small paper figure of Christ, or stick figure clothed like a shepherd; batting or cotton ball for reclining lamb (use white thread to tie around neck and shape head and ears; sew knots for eyes with black thread).*

Remember the story Jesus told about the lost sheep and the shepherd who worked so hard to find it? King David wrote a song about Jesus, the Good Shepherd. Every night we'll learn a new part of this psalm, and we'll build a picture box to help us remember the words.

The psalm begins like this: "The Lord is my shepherd, I shall not want" (Psalm 23:1, RSV).

Jesus is like our shepherd, and we are like His sheep. Jesus takes good care of us just as the good shepherd watched over his sheep.

"I shall not want" is a short way of saying "I will not want anything more, because I will already have everything I need." Jesus takes such good care of us that we don't need to worry about anything.

Let's make a place for our shepherd and the lamb to stand in our picture box. [Turn the box on its side and temporaily prop the shepherd and lamb.] ●

Theme: Jesus' Care

D
e
v
o
t
i
o
n

Green Pastures, Still Waters

He gives me rest in green pastures.
Psalm 23:2, ICB.

Materials: *mountain or meadow scenery for sides of box (calenders are good sources for scenery), green paper for grass (fringe strips and glue on green paper, pressing fringe up to look like grass around water, etc.), blue paper or fabric to create pool or stream, glue.*

R eview the first section of the shepherd's psalm.]

"He makes me lie down in green pastures. He leads me beside still waters" (Psalm 23:2, RSV).

Our shepherd, Jesus, knows that lambs need a peaceful place to rest, where there is plenty to eat and cool water to drink. He knows that kids like you need peaceful, loving places to grow up in too. You need plenty of good, healthful food and cool water.

Let's put some beautiful mountains and meadows around the side of our picture box, and grass and cool water in our picture box. Now let's find a nice place for Jesus the Shepherd and the lamb to stand.

We are Jesus' lambs, and He loves to take good care of us. He watches over us every day just as a shepherd watches over his sheep.

How many things can you think of that show us how well Jesus is caring for us?

Let's thank Jesus for being our good shepherd. ●

Theme: Jesus' Care

He Restores Us

He gives me new strength. Psalm 23:3, ICB.

Materials: *a rock, two to three inches in diameter, or a painted sponge; short, multi-branched twigs with paper leaves for bushes.*

Review first verses of the shepherd's psalm before going on.]
"He restores my soul" (Psalm 23:3, RSV).

Sometimes lambs get hot and tired. Then the shepherd finds a cool place for them to rest. Let's put a rock and some bushes in our picture box so the lamb will have a cool, safe place to rest.

Sometimes we get tired and cross, don't we? Sometimes we feel mad or sad. Jesus is our shepherd, and He helps us feel better. That's what "restores my soul" means.

Jesus reminds us that He will help us, whenever we have problems. We just need to pray and tell Him what we need.

Are there some things that are bothering you? Let's tell Jesus about them, and ask Him to help you feel better. Jesus is our shepherd, and He loves to help us with our problems.

You don't even have to stop and kneel to pray. Any time during the day that you think of Jesus, you can ask Him to "restore your soul." He will always hear you and help you. ●

Theme: Jesus' Care

#68

Paths of Righteousness

He leads me on paths that are right.
Psalm 23:3, ICB.

Materials: *pieces of gray paper, cut to look like*
stepping-stones; glue.

 eview first verses of the shepherd's
psalm with your child before con-
tinuing.]

"He leads me in paths of righteousness
for his name's sake" (Psalm 23:3, RSV).

Our shepherd knows all the best paths
through the fields and the mountains. He
knows the safest way to go to find the best
water and the nicest grass.

Jesus knows what kids need to do to be
safe and happy too. He helps us find the best
way by giving us Bible stories and giving us
rules about the right way to do things.

Let's cut out some stepping-stones to
make a path of righteousness in our picture
box. On each stone we'll write down a good
idea Jesus gives us to help us find the good
way. [Suggestions: pray, obey Mom and
Dad, tell the truth, share, don't steal, think
about Jesus' love, sing about Him, etc.]

When we walk in the path Jesus wants
us to walk in, we do the things He wants
us to do. We are doing it for Him, for His
name's sake. And we do it because we
know that Jesus knows what will make
us happy. ●

#69

Theme: Obedience

Valley of the Shadow

Even if I walk through a very dark valley, I will not be afraid. Psalm 23:4, ICB.

Materials: *black paper, crumpled into cloud shape, hanging from ceiling of box; bright-yellow paper or pipe cleaner, shaped like lightning; sticks for a rod and staff.*

Even though Jesus wants us to be safe and happy, sometimes bad things happen. Sometimes it rains when you want to play outside. Or you get sick and have to miss something fun. Sometimes people we love get very sick. [Depending on child's maturity discuss relevent specifics. Put up the dark cloud and lightning in corner of box.]

What kinds of things scare you? [Parent, you share childhood fears.] It's OK to feel scared. Lambs get frightened too. When we are frightened, we can think of our Good Shepherd. Our psalm says, "Even though I walk through the valley of the shadow of death, I will fear no evil, for you are with me; your rod and your staff, they comfort me" (Psalm 23:4, NIV). We know that even when scary things happen, Jesus is always near. [Play act the "shepherd" helping sheep.]

We can always trust Him to take care of us. Even if you should get hurt, you know Jesus is with you, and He will comfort you. "Remember," Jesus says, "that I am your good shepherd. I always take care of My sheep." ●

Theme: Trust

#70

A Table Spread for Us

You prepare a meal for me in front of my enemies. Psalm 23:5, ICB.

Materials: *a 2" x 2" square of fringed cloth (tablecloth), grain, small pictures or plastic figures of wild animals, such as a wolf and a bear.*

Review previous verses of psalm.] "You prepare a table before me in the presence of my enemies" (Psalm 23:5, NIV).

Here Jesus, our good shepherd, is doing something fun! He is having a picnic with His lamb! They are having a picnic, even though there are all kinds of enemies around. Here is a wolf that would love to catch a little lamb. Here is a bear, waiting for the lamb to come along. [Place these animals around the edge of the scene.]

"Don't worry," Jesus tells His little lamb. [Spread the "tablecloth" on the rock or grass.] "I know there are wolves and bears out there that want to eat you. But they can't, because I'm here to watch over you. Here's some tasty grain. I believe I'll have some Myself. It's too bad those wolves and bears don't like bread!"

What a funny picnic! You know, when Jesus makes our world over new, the bears and wolves *will* eat grain and grass, for there won't be any killing in the new earth. We can have picnics with them! Until then, though, Jesus knows how to take care of us. ●

#71

Theme: Jesus' Care

My Cup, Full and Running Over

You give me more than I can hold. Psalm 23:5, ICB.

Materials: *cup, food (dry cornmeal or rice), oil, tiny cup for picture box.*

You anoint my head with oil; my cup overflows" (Psalm 23:5, NIV).

Sometimes a sheep's face got scratched by thorn bushes. The shepherd "anointed" or poured oil on its head to make the scratches feel better. Do you want to see how nice oil feels to your skin? [Pour a little baby oil or cooking oil on your child's hands.] How does that feel?

The Bible often describes blessings as being like oil that is poured out in a full, rich amount. Jesus gives us so many blessings that if there were a cup to hold them, the blessings would run over the cup. [Let your child hold a cup. Pour oil, cornmeal, or rice into cup, letting them experience it pouring over their hands. Put a small cup on the "tablecloth" in the box.]

Jesus gives us so many blessings; He gives us more than we can hold. Our cup runs over. Just think of the good things that we have. More flowers than we can ever see. More water than we can ever drink. More birds to sing and make the world beautiful, and more music than we can ever hear. How much Jesus loves us! ●

Theme: Blessings

The House of the Lord

Surely your goodness and love will be with me all my life. Psalm 23:6, ICB.

Materials: *a rainbow made out of poster board, large enough to cover the sides and top of the opening of the box; glitter; heart stickers. If the box is dark, cut slits wide enough to let in light through the top of the box.*

eview previous verses with your child.]

"Surely goodness and mercy shall follow me all the days of my life; and I shall dwell in the house of the Lord for ever" (Psalm 23:6).

When Jesus is our shepherd and we are with Him every day, each day is more and more like living in heaven. Jesus' goodness and His loving mercy comfort us when we are sad or scared. Jesus protects us from hurtful things. And as we live closer and closer to Jesus, heaven starts here on earth for us.

Someday Jesus is coming to take us to His home in heaven, and there'll be no more sad, scary things. We won't have any more enemies. Jesus promises us that we'll live in His house forever! What a wonderful promise!

Put this glittery rainbow over the sides and top of your box to remind us of this promise. We'll put hearts on the rainbow, with the words "Goodness" and "Mercy" written on them, to remind us that life with our Shepherd Jesus is good, and heaven starts here. [Now say the whole psalm together.] ●

Theme: Second Coming

The Blind Men

"Lord, we want to be able to see."
Matthew 20:33, ICB.

Materials: *blindfold, cookie, toothbrush,*
toothpaste.

I'm going to tie this blindfold around your eyes and lead you through the house. [Lead child around corners, up and down stairs. In the kitchen, have a snack for child to eat. Then lead child to the bathroom. Let child feel for toothbrush and brush teeth, still blindfolded. Remove blindfold; discuss how it felt not to see.]

Listen to this story about two blind men. [Read Matthew 20:29-34.]

Jesus was very sorry for these two men. He healed their eyes so they could see. But He was also thinking of people who could see with their eyes—but they were blind in other ways. They couldn't see how much Jesus loved them and wanted to help them live happy lives.

Jesus wanted to open these people's eyes too, but they didn't feel that they were blind, and they didn't want Jesus' help. This made Jesus even more sorry. He could help the blind men, but He couldn't help the people who didn't want His help.

Let's ask Jesus to open our eyes so we can see how much we need Him. Then He can help us live good, happy lives!

Theme: Salvation

#74

Grandmother's Fixed-up Back

"Woman, your sickness has left you!"
Luke 13:12, ICB.

Materials: *using large handkerchief, two buttons, thread or marker, make an "old woman" puppet: tie handkerchief around fist for a scarf. Make eyes with a marker or two buttons tied together by thread. Your thumb, moving up and down, is the old woman's mouth. [Let her tell the story.]*

ello, children. I feel so good today! I thank God over and over. Do you want to know why I feel so good? I'll tell you. My back used to be all bent over. Can you walk all bent over? Try it. It's hard, isn't it! Oh, my back hurt so much, and I had to walk with a stick.

Well, one day I heard that Jesus was coming to our church, and that He healed people. I wanted to be able to stand up straight, and I wanted my back to stop hurting. So I grabbed up my walking stick and hobbled to the church on Sabbath.

When Jesus saw me, He said, "You are rid of your trouble" (Luke 13:12, REB). And then He put His hands on me. All of a sudden, there I was, standing straight and tall, and my back didn't hurt a bit! "Thank You, thank You, thank You, God, for sending Jesus to make me well!" I said over and over.

Some men at church were angry because Jesus healed me on the Sabbath. But Jesus said it was right for me to be freed of my trouble on the Sabbath. It was the happiest Sabbath I ever had! You can help me praise God. Say Praise God! Thank You, Jesus! ●

#75

Theme: Healing

Perfume Bottle

So she brought an alabaster jar of perfume. Luke 7:37, ICB.

Materials: *perfume.*

One night Jesus went to supper at Simon's house. As Jesus ate, a woman named Mary crept into the dining room. Silently she knelt at Jesus' feet. She was crying and, as she kissed Jesus' feet, her tears got His feet wet. So she shook out her long hair and wiped the tears away. Then she took a beautiful bottle of perfume and poured it out on Jesus' feet. Suddenly everyone who had been busy eating looked around. They smelled the sweet perfume, and they saw the woman at Jesus' feet.

If Jesus knew what a bad woman she is, He wouldn't let her touch Him! Simon thought.

But Jesus did know all about Mary, who was crying at His feet. He said, "Her many sins are forgiven. This is clear because she showed great love. But the person who has only a little to be forgiven will feel only a little love" (Luke 7:47, ICB).

No one is so bad that we can't come to Jesus. If we ask, He will forgive us.

Smell this perfume; put some on yourself. As you smell its sweetness throughout the day, think of the goodness of Jesus, and of how Mary showed her love for Him. ●

Theme: Forgiveness

#76

Sheep Without a Shepherd

They were like sheep without a shepherd.
Matthew 9:36, ICB.

Materials: *clothespins, cotton or stuffing,*
heavy paper. Method: Cut a four-
inch oval shape from heavy paper.
Cut a smaller oval for sheep's head;
glue to body. Clip two clothespins to
body for legs and glue cotton on
body and legs. Perhaps tie a ribbon
and bell around neck.

Remember the crowds who listened to Jesus up on the mountain? And remember all the people who pressed in on Jesus when Jairus wanted Him to help his dying daughter? As Jesus went to the villages preaching and healing, people crowded everywhere. Jesus felt sorry for them. "They were harassed and help-less, like sheep without a shepherd" (Matthew 9:36, NIV).

Jesus said that the crowds were like sheep. When any little problem comes up, sheep need shepherds to protect them. The people knew Jesus would help them. He is the Good Shepherd. But Jesus needs helpers to help Him take care of the people.

Would you like to be Jesus' helper? He is the Master Shepherd, and each one of us can be His undershepherds. You and I can love everyone, just as Jesus does. We should feel sad for those who are poor and have problems. We should help them.

Do you know anyone Jesus would like you to help Him shepherd?

To remind you that Jesus needs your help, you can make a sheep. ●

Theme: Service

Give Without Charge

"Heal the sick. . . . I give you these powers freely." Matthew 10:8, ICB.

Materials: *notebook, pencil.*

Jesus had done a lot of teaching and preaching and healing. Now it was time to teach His friends how to do this work, for He would be gone soon. As each person taught another one, how quickly everyone in the country would know about Jesus' kingdom!

"I want you to heal the sick, raise the dead, cleanse the lepers, and drive out evil spirits," Jesus said. Jesus' friends were to do all that! And Jesus added, "You received all my help without paying any money; give your help without charging people money."

Jesus, the most expensive gift heaven ever gave, was free to us: All the money in the world, piled up in huge mountains, could never pay God back for sending Jesus to save our world. Even though we could never pay enough, God gave Him to us anyway.

[Take a walk and look for other free gifts. Write them down, or draw pictures of them.] Jesus wants us to give just as He gives—without charging money or any other price. What free gifts can you give? [Discuss this: love, smiles, stories of Jesus, kind deeds, etc.] ●

Theme: Service

#78

Do Not Be Afraid

"So don't be afraid of those people."
Matthew 10:26, ICB.

Materials: *storybook, or storytelling cards.*

Jesus told His friends not to be afraid when they went out to tell people about Him. "The things I tell you in the dark," Jesus said, "you must tell others in broad daylight; what you hear Me whisper, you must shout." Sometimes it takes practice to be brave enough to speak to people about Jesus. But remember Jesus said, "Do not be afraid." [Try these easy games to practice communication skills:

[**Whisper and Shout.** One person whispers something about Jesus to someone; that someone crosses to the other side of the room and shouts out what they heard. Take turns.

[**Storytelling.** Tell a short story to your child, using pictures or a storybook. Then let your child tell the story to your family. Have a storytelling night once a week; each person tells something learned about Jesus that week.

[**Who's in Charge.** Each person in your family takes turns being in charge of family worship. You can help the child plan the activities, but the child should lead—call the family together, instruct them in the activities, etc.] ●

#79

Theme: Witnessing

When Sparrows Fall

'God even knows how many hairs are on your head. So don't be afraid. You are worth much more than many birds."
Matthew 10:30, ICB.

Materials: *marker, hair clips.*

One spring the robins came back to our town before all the snow was gone from the fields. Robins tried to find worms where the snowplows had cleared the sides of the road. Many of them were weak, and when they tried to fly up away from the cars, they got confused and flew into the cars instead.

Jesus said something very comforting: "How much does it cost to buy two sparrows? Just one penny! But not one of these sparrows falls to the ground without your Father knowing all about it." Then Jesus said, "The Father knows all about you, too—He has counted even the hairs on your head!"

Let's try counting the hairs on your head. [With a marker, draw a quarter-inch square on the scalp. Keep other hair away with hair clips.] Can you count all the hairs in the colored square? [Measure head with a tape measure; estimate how many quarter-inch squares are on head. Then calculate how many hairs on head.] It's pretty hard to count every hair!

Does this help you understand just a little how much God cares for you? ●

Theme: God's Care

I Know Jesus

"If anyone stands before other people and says he believes in me, then I will say that he belongs to me. I will say this before my Father in heaven." Matthew 10:32, ICB.

Activity: *role play.*

P eter was scared. It was dark, and Jesus had been arrested. They wanted to crucify Him. Peter was afraid they would hurt him too, because he was Jesus' friend. Peter stayed near Jesus, but he was too scared to let anybody know they were friends.

"Hey, don't you hang around with this Jesus guy?" people called out to Peter.

"No! No! I don't know Jesus," Peter lied.

Jesus turned to look at Peter. Jesus looked so sad that Peter ran out and cried and cried. And of course, Jesus forgave him.

After that Peter told everyone that Jesus was his friend, even when Peter was put in jail for being a Christian.

Jesus is your friend. And when someone is your friend, it's important to stick up for him or her, even when others are saying mean things about them.

[Role play.] What would you do if some-one asked *you,* "Are you one of those silly people who pray and go to church?" or "What good is Jesus, anyway? Why do you love Him?" ●

#81

Theme: Loyalty

Jesus' Cross

"No one is worthy of me who does not take up his cross and follow me."
Matthew 10:38, REB.

Materials: *sticks, six to 10 inches long; string. Method: make a simple cross by tying sticks together in shape of a cross.*

Once I saw a man walking beside the road, pulling a cross on wheels. He was walking across the country with his cross. When people asked what he was doing, he would tell them about Jesus. Dragging a real cross wherever he went and talking about Jesus was this man's way of following Jesus. Can you think of other ways?

Jesus loved us so much that He died for us. To pick up our cross means to care more about loving people and helping Jesus in His work than anything else.

The way you play, the way you talk to your mom and dad and brothers and sisters, the way you help with housework and yard work, all show if Jesus is really important to you.

[Have each person in the family make a simple cross. Choose one day during which each one will carry their cross everywhere— work, shopping, playing, washing dishes. In the evening ask how keeping the cross with them all day made them feel. What did they think? Did they do anything differently? Did others ask about the cross?] ●

Theme: Service

#82

A Cup of Cold Water

"Whoever helps one of these little ones because they are my followers will truly get his reward. He will get his reward even if he only gave my follower a cup of cold water." Matthew 10:42, ICB.

Materials: *paper, pencils.*

J esus has many friends who are His helpers. Can you think of anybody who is Jesus' helper? Your Sabbath school teachers are helpers, aren't they? [Discuss other people your child knows, such as pastor, grandparents, or anyone who helps teach us what's right.]

Jesus said we should treat His helpers just as we would treat Him. "Whoever helps one of these little ones because they are my followers will truly get his reward, even if he only gave my follower a cup of cold water."

Children who love and follow Jesus are special! Jesus says that giving His special friends a drink of cool water will be rewarded!

Can you think of anything nice to do for any of Jesus' helpers you know? [Name some of Jesus' helpers known to family.] You could make a thank-you card, fruit bread, or something else special, or you could just tell them thank you the next time you see them. What would you like to do? Remember, treat them as you would treat Jesus.

Theme: Service

If You Have Ears

"You people who hear me, listen!"
Matthew 11:15, ICB.

Materials: *pink paper, scissors.*

While Jesus was busy traveling among the towns, healing and preaching, John the Baptist was in jail. King Herod had done something wrong, and John the Baptist had told him it was wrong. That had made King Herod very angry. So John sat in the jail looking through the bars and wondering about Jesus.

John's friends came to Jesus. "John is wondering if You are really the One we are looking for," they said.

Jesus showed them all the people He was healing. "The poor are brought good news," He said (Matthew 11:5, REB). "Go tell John about all the good things you've seen."

Then as John's friends hurried back to the jail, Jesus talked to the people about John. He told them that John the Baptist was a great prophet of God, but people hadn't listened to him. "If you have ears, then hear," Jesus said (verse 15, REB).

Cut out a big ear and put it where it will remind you to listen to Jesus.

Theme: Listening

#84

"Take My Yoke"

"Come to me, all of you who are tired and have heavy loads. I will give you rest." Matthew 11:28, ICB.

Materials: *rags, string, picture of Jesus, or stick cross (see 82).*

As Jesus talked to poor people, day after day, He saw many who were tired and worried. Dads worked hard on the fishing boats and in the fields, but they were worried that their families wouldn't have enough food or enough clothes or a good place to live.

Do you ever get tired and worried and afraid? [Discuss your child's worries and fears in an open, accepting way.] Jesus said, "Come to me, all who are weary and whose load is heavy; I will give you rest" (Matthew 11:28, REB).

Sometimes being scared makes us tired. But when we listen to the things Jesus tells us, our hearts can rest. We will know that He loves us, just the way we are. "I will give you rest," Jesus says. Think about that as you go to sleep.

[Make a big bundle of rags or paper and wrap it with string.] Imagine that this bundle holds all your worries and fears. Let's lay it under a picture of Jesus (or the stick cross). ●

#85

Theme: Worry

Lord of the Sabbath

"The Son of Man is Lord of the Sabbath day." Matthew 12:8, ICB.

Materials: *two cardboard tubes, paper, yarn. [To make tassel: cut 20 8-inch pieces of yarn. Bundle them, and tie the bundle in the middle. Bend yarn in half, and wrap bundle several times near the folded end.]*

One Sabbath Jesus and His friends were walking through a field of grain. Some of the men picked a few heads of grain and began eating them. "Your friends aren't keeping Sabbath the right way," the priests said to Jesus. "They are harvesting grain!"

"I wouldn't want My friends to go hungry on the Sabbath," Jesus replied. "The Sabbath is a day to help people, not hurt them. And I know, because I *made* the Sabbath day."

You can make a Sabbath scroll. Take two cardboard paper towel rolls. Slit them lengthwise, and roll each one tighter. Glue them closed. Use rubber bands to secure them until the glue sets.

On a sheet of paper write "Jesus is Lord of the Sabbath." Decorate the page with a picture, drawing, or bright colors. Glue one of the cardboard rolls at the top of the sheet of paper, and the other at the bottom of your sheet of paper. Make gold tassels out of yarn and tie one at each end of the top of your scroll. To make a hanger, use a piece of yarn running from tassel to tassel. Now you can hang your scroll up. ●

Theme: Sabbath

#86

Doing Good on the Sabbath

"So the law of Moses allows people to do good things on the Sabbath day."
Matthew 12:12, ICB.

Materials: *two cardboard paper towel tubes, paper, yarn, glue.*

When Jesus went to church one day, He saw a man with a withered arm. The priests were trying to make trouble for Jesus. They wanted to catch Him doing something wrong. They thought that if Jesus healed this man they could tell everyone He was doing something that was wrong to do on the Sabbath.

But Jesus couldn't walk by anyone who was hurting without wanting to help. "If your sheep fell into a ditch on the Sabbath," He said, "wouldn't you help it out? This man is worth more than any sheep. It is right to do good on the Sabbath."

So Jesus said to the man, "Stretch out your arm."

As soon as the man did, his withered arm became as good as new.

What good do you like to do on the Sabbath? [Discuss this.]

You can make a companion scroll to yesterday's Sabbath scroll. Follow the same instructions, but this time write on the paper, "It is right to do good on the Sabbath." You may also draw pictures of the good things you like to do on the Sabbath. ●

#87

Theme: Sabbath

God Says, "I Love You"

"Here is my servant whom I have chosen. I love him, and I am pleased with him." Matthew 12:18, ICB.

Materials: *red and white paper, doilies, lace, flowers, etc., for making valentines.*

J esus often talked about the Bible verses, written long before, that told about His coming. He wanted the people to remember that God had planned for Him to come, and He came just at the right time.

Did you know that God has a plan for you too? He has something special for you to do.

This is what a prophet said about Jesus. "Here is my servant whom I have chosen, the one I love . . . ; I will put my Spirit on him" (Matthew 12:18, NIV). This verse is like a valentine from God to Jesus. God the Father and Jesus the Son loved each other so much. But they loved us too, so Jesus became a servant to help us. He showed us what justice and right was like, and He helps it happen. Jesus is beloved of God. And God sent His beloved Jesus to us because He loves us too. Jesus is like God's valentine to us that says, "Be Mine. I love you."

You can make valentines with red and white paper. Make a valentine from God to Jesus, and another one from God to us. And make an extra-special valentine from you to God! ●

Theme: God's Goodness

88

A Smoldering Wick

"He will not argue or shout." **Matthew 12:19, ICB.**

Materials: *candle; matches; reed; grass stem or twig, almost broken in half.*

Isaiah, a prophet, said something very interesting about the way Jesus would work: "He will not quarrel or cry out. . . . A bruised reed he will not break, and a smoldering wick he will not snuff out" (Matthew 12:19, 20, NIV).

Here's a broken stem. It would be really easy to break it off! But Jesus didn't do that. He left it alone.

Here's a candle. We'll light it and let it burn for a few minutes. If we just blow lightly, the flame will go out, but the wick still smolders and smokes. Usually we pinch the wick to make it stop smoking. But not Jesus. He didn't even make a candle stop burning.

This is an example of how Jesus treats us. He doesn't force us to do things His way. He lets us think about what we really want to do, even if it takes a long time. It might take a long time for this broken stem to fall off by itself, or for this candle to quit smoking. But Jesus is willing to wait. That's how kindly and gently He treats us. He is waiting patiently for us to decide that we really want to go to heaven with Him. ●

#89

Theme: Jesus is like . . .

Jesus Saves!

"Every family that is divided cannot succeed." Matthew 12:25, ICB.

Materials: *roll of paper, or 10 sheets; tape; potato; tempera paint. [To decorate banner: use tempera paint and a stamp cut from a potato in the shape of a star or heart.]*

 any of the priests and teachers in the towns Jesus visited didn't like Him. He was too different. But the regular *people* liked Jesus. "Oh, look!" the people cried. "Jesus healed this blind man. He can see!"

"That's because Jesus uses Satan's power to drive out the devils that made the man blind," the jealous priests and teachers said.

"Why would Satan drive out his own devils?" Jesus asked. "No one can take something away from someone as strong as Satan unless that person ties him up first."

Jesus is much stronger than Satan, and that's wonderful news! We don't have to be afraid of any power Satan has, because Jesus saves us!

[Make a banner announcing this good news! Use paper that comes on a roll, or tape 9 or 10 sheets together. Write "Jesus Saves!" in big colorful letters and decorate the banner.] ●

Theme: Salvation

#90

Working With Jesus

"If anyone is not with me, then he is against me." Matthew 12:30, ICB.

Materials: *toy box or basket full of small blocks or other toys.*

Some priests and teachers were jealous of Jesus and were hurting His work. They said they loved God, but they didn't like Jesus. Jesus said He loved God and that His power was from God. Who was telling the truth?

Jesus didn't want the people to be confused by the lies the priests and teachers were telling. "He who is not with me is against me," Jesus said, "and he who does not gather with me scatters" (Matthew 12:30, REB).

Have you ever tried to rake up leaves while someone was running through them, scattering them? [Discuss.] Let's pretend your toys are all over the floor, and you're trying to put them away. [Scatter the toys, and let child start putting them away.] Now I come in and start scattering them. I'm making it hard for you to clean up. How do you feel? You would feel much better if I helped you, wouldn't you? I'll help you now! [Put toys away.]

I want to help Jesus do good things for people, don't you? What good things should we do today? ●

71

Theme: Service

The Holy Spirit

"Anyone who says things against the Holy Spirit will not be forgiven." Matthew 12:32, ICB.

Materials: *bright-colored felt or craft foam, scissors, puffy fabric paint.*

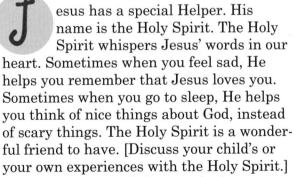

J esus has a special Helper. His name is the Holy Spirit. The Holy Spirit whispers Jesus' words in our heart. Sometimes when you feel sad, He helps you remember that Jesus loves you. Sometimes when you go to sleep, He helps you think of nice things about God, instead of scary things. The Holy Spirit is a wonderful friend to have. [Discuss your child's or your own experiences with the Holy Spirit.]

When the Holy Spirit speaks in our hearts, we should always listen carefully. If we keep shutting Him out, a time will come when we will never want to be close to God, and the Holy Spirit will leave us alone to do what we choose.

We can make a welcome mat to remind us always to welcome the Holy Spirit's quiet words in our heart. [Snip the edges of the felt for a fringe, or cut it with pinking shears. Cut pieces of felt or craft foam to glue on the felt. Use felt letters or write with a puffy fabric paint, "Welcome, Holy Spirit."] ●

Theme: Holy Spirit ✂

#92

Words From the Heart

"The mouth speaks the things that are in the heart." Matthew 12:34, ICB.

Materials: *tape recorder, video camera, or answering machine.*

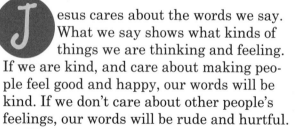

Jesus cares about the words we say. What we say shows what kinds of things we are thinking and feeling. If we are kind, and care about making people feel good and happy, our words will be kind. If we don't care about other people's feelings, our words will be rude and hurtful.

[Try this activity if you have access to a tape recorder or some other means of recording a voice.] What kinds of words do you like to hear? How do you like people's voices to sound when they talk to you? Let's say some nice things on the tape recorder

and see how they sound. [Let your child record this, if possible.] How do you feel when you say nice things? How do you feel when you hear them?

When do we have trouble with words in our family? [Discuss being tired, hungry, rushed, etc.] How can we have better thoughts and feelings during these times so our words will still be kind? If Jesus is in our hearts, He will help our words be kind. ●

Theme: Words

Thoughtless Words

"I tell you that people will have to explain about every careless thing they have said." Matthew 12:36, ICB.

Materials: *tape recorder, cassette with prerecorded family conversations during mealtime, playtime, etc.*

It's easy to say words. Words don't cost us anything, and they disappear into thin air as soon as we say them! Well, it seems as if they disappear, because we never see them. But our words don't really disappear. We can record our words and God can keep track of our words too.

Jesus said, "I'm telling you that you will have to explain why you said every thoughtless word when the time comes for judgment."

God knows how much our words can help others—or hurt them. We should be very careful with the words we use.

[Play recording of family. Discuss the recording.] What good things did you hear on our tape? Did you hear anything that made you feel badly?

Sometimes we need to ask Jesus to forgive us for careless, hurtful words we've said. Jesus will clean our record. We should ask people to whom we spoke unkindly to forgive us as well. Then we can ask Jesus to stay in our hearts and help us speak good words to each other. ●

Theme: Words

#94

Greater Than Jonah and Solomon

"I tell you that someone greater than Jonah is here!" Matthew 12:41, ICB.

Materials: *pinking shears, small picture of Jesus, tacky glue, felt, safety pin. [Method: Cut out the picture in a circle. Glue to felt. With shears, cut around felt. Glue safety pin on felt back.]*

Can you remember the things in our stories that Jesus has been doing to help people? [Discuss.] In spite of all the good things Jesus was doing, some men pretended that they still didn't know whether Jesus was from God. "Teacher," they said, "show us a sign that you are from God."

Some people just don't want to believe in Jesus, and it doesn't matter what He does, or what you and I do to help them. People who think too much of themselves sometimes have trouble like this. *I am very smart,* they think. *I don't need Jesus.*

Remember Jonah? [Review this story quickly.] The people in Nineveh believed his message was from God. And once the queen of Sheba visited King Solomon. She knew King Solomon's wisdom was from God.

"I who am with you now," Jesus said, "am greater than Jonah and greater than King Solomon." Jesus is God with us. [Discuss how you know God is with you.] ●

Theme: Listening

Jesus Is Knocking

"Here I am! I stand at the door and knock." Revelation 3:20, ICB.

Materials: *dollhouse, miniature set of dishes, table or pictures of dishes and table, figure of Jesus, figure of child.*

esus said, "Here I am, standing at your door and knocking. If you hear My voice and open the door, I will come in, and we will eat together."

[Set up dishes and table in dollhouse, and have your "child" doll sit down with the "Jesus" doll (or use pictures or a real place setting at your own table with a place marked "Jesus").]

Why do you think Jesus wants to eat with us in our house? What happens when our family eats together? [Discuss the good times, good conversations, closeness, etc.]

Jesus wants to spend times like that with us! He wants to talk with us and listen to us. He wants to feel close to us. It's a special "togetherness" feeling.

When we are together during family worship and we invite Jesus to be with us, it's like inviting Jesus to eat with us! What are some other times when we feel close to Jesus? [Discuss personal prayer, church, etc.] ●

Theme: Jesus, Our Friend ✎

My Brother and Sister and Mother

"My true brothers and sisters and mother are those who do the things that my Father in heaven wants." Matthew 12:50, ICB.

Materials: *cardboard cut into wreath shape, old* National Geographic *magazines, an old children's quarterly, family pictures, glue, scissors.*

J esus was speaking to crowds of people when someone touched His arm. "Your mother and brothers have come, and they're waiting to talk to you," the man said.

Jesus was glad to know His mother and brothers were there, because He loved them. But Jesus had come to our world to be a brother to all of us. "Who is my mother? Who are my brothers?" He asked. Then He pointed to His friends. "Here are my mother and my brothers. Whoever does the will of my heavenly Father in heaven is my brother and sister and mother" (Matthew 12:48-50, REB).

When we listen to God and obey Him as our heavenly Father, we are all family, together with Jesus. We have brothers and sisters all over the world! You can make a family wreath. Cut out pictures of people from all over the world. [The *National Geographic* is a good source of pictures.] Include a picture of Jesus and pictures of your family.

Glue the pictures onto a cardboard shaped like a wreath. You can call this "Our Family." ●

#97

Theme: Family

The Footpath

"While he was planting, some seed fell by the road." Matthew 13:4, ICB.

Materials: *plastic cups, hard-packed dirt, seed (large bean), heart stickers for outside of cups.*

J esus went down to the lake where the water lapped peacefully and the warm sun shone. So many people gathered around Him that He got into a little fishing boat and sat there while He told His stories. The children looked up and saw a farmer on a hill nearby, scattering seed over the ground.

"Some of the seed fell on the path where people walk," Jesus said. "Some fell on rocky soil. Some fell in among the thistles and weeds. And some fell on good soil." Jesus told this story to help His friends learn about how His words grow in people's hearts.

The different kinds of dirt are like different kinds of people. Let's take these little plastic cups and fill them with the different kinds of dirt Jesus talked about. Let's press down the dirt in our first cup—we have to make it hard, like the footpath. What kind of people are "hard" like this dirt? [Discuss.]

What happened to the seeds that fell on the footpath? The birds ate it up before it even had a chance to grow. We don't want to be like that. [Discuss.] ●

Theme: Listening

Devotion

The Rocky Soil

"That seed is like the person who hears the teaching and quickly accepts it with joy." Matthew 13:20, ICB.

Materials: *clear plastic cups with heart stickers on outside, rocks, seeds (soaked overnight).*

Yesterday we talked about the farmer who was scattering his seed. Some of it fell on rocky soil. While Jesus was telling this story, the children playing along the lakeshore looked down at the rocky beach. Nothing would grow for very long among the rocks. Little sprouts would dry up quickly under the hot sun. There's no dirt to keep the seeds damp and cool, and so the sprouts soon die.

Let's fill our second cup with rocks and pebbles. We can sprinkle seeds in among the rocks and water them. Then we'll see how well they grow. Jesus said the rocky ground was like some of the people who listened to Him. These people liked Jesus, but they thought about His words for only a few minutes, then forget all about them. When there was trouble, they didn't use Jesus' words to help them. And so Jesus' words died in their hearts, like the sprouts among the rocks.

I don't want my heart to be hard or rocky, do you? I want Jesus' words to grow in my heart. ●

#99

Theme: Listening

Among the Thistles

"That seed is like the person who hears the teaching but lets worries about this life and love of money stop that teaching from growing." Matthew 13:22, ICB.

Materials: *clear plastic cup with heart stickers on outside, seeds (soaked overnight), weedy soil, picture of (or real) thistles.*

We're ready to fill our third cup. Remember what we have in our first two cups? What kind of person is our first cup like? [People who don't like Jesus.] What kind of people have hearts like the rocky soil in this cup? [People who don't listen to what Jesus says. Discuss.]

Jesus said that some of the seeds the farmer scattered fell in soil where thistles were already growing. Thistles have pretty fluffy flowers. [Find the real flower, or show a picture.] Thistles grow very close together. No other plant can live among this-tles. The thistles spread out and take everything other little sprouts need to grow.

Jesus said that some people worry so much that they don't have time to think about His words. Jesus' lessons can't grow very big in their minds, because other things choke them out.

Let's put this weedy soil in our cup. Then we'll plant our seeds and see what happens. This is a poor place to plant seeds. But this lesson helps us think about our hearts. Do we have weeds growing that choke out thoughts of Jesus? ●

Theme: Listening

#100

Good Soil

"That seed is like the person who hears the teaching and understands it."
Matthew 13:23, ICB.

Materials: *clear plastic cup, potting soil, fast-sprouting seeds (soaked overnight).*

At last it's time to plant our seeds in good soil! Did you like planting seeds in the other cups? [Seeds couldn't grow. Discuss.] The last soil Jesus talked about was just right for the seeds. There was plenty of sunshine and water for the growing plants. It's nice to know that the seeds we'll plant today have a good chance of growing healthy and strong. Jesus said, "The seed sown on good soil is the person who hears the word and understands it" (Matthew 13:23, REB). "That person grows and produces fruit" (verse 23, ICB).

These people listen carefully to Jesus, and they think about what He says until they understand what He wants them to do. Then they do it. And as they obey Jesus, they become nicer and nicer. They want to help others, too. All the good things they do are like growing all kinds of good fruit from the seed Jesus planted in their hearts.

This is the kind of person I want to be, don't you? Jesus is the good farmer. We can ask Him to make our hearts soft, to take bad things out of our hearts so it will be easy to plant His good lessons in our hearts. ●

Theme: Listening

The Wheat and the Weeds

"The kingdom of heaven is like a man who planted good seed in his field."
Matthew 13:24, ICB.

Materials: *large sheet of paper, markers. [Help child draw a clock. Draw farmer sowing seed at 3:00; enemy sowing seeds at 6:00; wheat and weeds together at 9:00; a fire burning weeds at 12:00.]*

Jesus said that once a farmer sowed good wheat seed in his field. But during the night an enemy sowed bad seeds in with the good seeds. When the seeds started growing, they were so mixed up that if the farmer pulled up the bad plants, the wheat would come up, too.

So the good farmer told his helpers, "Let both the weeds and the wheat grow together. When it's time to harvest the wheat, I will tell the reapers, 'Gather the weeds first and tie them in bundles so they can be burned. Then collect the wheat into my barn.'"

"I'm the farmer," Jesus explained. "The wheat stands for the people who do good. When I come, I'll take them to heaven."

The weeds stand for those who hurt others. [Discuss any experiences your child brings up about things that trouble him or her about their world.] Jesus wants us to be happy and safe. All the troubles in this world make Him sad too. This story tells us that when the time is right, Jesus will burn all the evil things in our world and make it a wonderful, happy place to live again. Jesus always does things at the right time. ●

Theme: Judgment

#102

Shining Like the Sun

"Then the good people will shine like the sun in the kingdom of their Father." Matthew 13:43, ICB.

Materials: *yellow marker, picture of child.*

Let's take another look at Jesus' time clock. Can you tell me the story about the good farmer, and what happened to his field of wheat? [Let your child tell you this story, using the pictures as an aid.] It will be such a happy time when Jesus comes to take all those who love Him to heaven. I want to be in the good harvest.

Jesus said, "Then the good people will shine like the sun in the kingdom of their Father." That's where I want to be! Jesus says we will be so happy we will shine like the sun!

Even though we sometimes do wrong, when we ask Jesus, He forgives our sins. And He helps us *want* to do right. I'm so glad Jesus came to save us from our sins. Let's thank Him for loving us and ask Him to forgive us for our sins and make us good like Him. [Pray with your child.]

You can make a beautiful shining sun and glue your picture in the center of the sun. Then glue your shining sun on Jesus' time clock. ●

Theme: Judgment

The Mustard Seed

"The kingdom of heaven is like a mustard seed." Matthew 13:31, ICB.

Jesus gathered the children around Him to tell them stories. They always loved His stories. Maybe He had some seeds in His hand to show them—tiny, tiny seeds.

"I'm going to tell you a story about these seeds," Jesus said. "The kingdom of heaven is like one little mustard seed that a farmer plants in his field. This seed is smaller than any other seed he plants, but when it grows, it becomes taller than all the other plants! It makes big branches too. It's so big that the birds come and roost among its branches."

Jesus was trying to explain what the kingdom of heaven is like. Nobody can see the kingdom of heaven. It is like a seed planted in someone's heart—that's not something you can see. But Jesus' words in our hearts grow into something big enough for everyone to see.

[Discuss how we change when we follow Jesus. Discuss good deeds.]

Theme: Heaven

#104

God's Kingdom on Earth

"Though it is the smallest of all your seeds . . . [it] becomes a tree."
Matthew 13:32, NIV.

Materials: *big towel (to throw off as seed grows in pantomine).*

Yesterday we talked about the mustard seed and how it grows into such a big tree that birds make nests in its branches. This reminds us that when God's word is planted in our hearts, we change and everyone can see how we change.

Everyone can see the kind things we do for others. They can see that we are Jesus' friends. The kingdom of heaven starts here on earth, in people's hearts. Then, when it's time, Jesus will take everyone who loves Him to heaven to live with Him.

Let's act out how seeds grow. Roll up into a tiny seed, and I will cover you with this towel, just as the soil covers the seed. [Walk around your child, acting like rain.] God's rain comes down and soaks you till you swell and your little brown coat bursts open. [Throw off towel.] God's sun warms you up, and your little green sprout reaches higher and higher. [Child's hand starts to reach up.] It reaches up above the dirt to the sun. You grow to a tall tree [child stands], swaying in the breeze, and the birds come and sleep in your branches at night! [Your hands can be a bird, flying down to rest on your child's shoulders.] ●

#105

Theme: Growing in Jesus

Yeast

"The kingdom of heaven is like yeast."
Matthew 13:33, ICB.

Materials: *bread recipe, 1 package dry yeast, white flour, sugar or honey, salt, warm water, oil.*

Jesus told another story about what the kingdom of heaven is like.

"It's like yeast," Jesus said. "When you make bread, you mix a little bit of yeast in your dough. The yeast grows and grows and makes the whole batch of bread dough rise."

[Help child mix the yeast with 3 cups of warm water until it is dissolved. Add 2 tablespoons sugar or honey, 1 teaspoon salt, 3 tablespoons oil, and enough flour to make a soupy dough. Cover, and let it rise in a warm place for an hour or so. As child stirs the mass, talk about the little bubbles of gas the yeast made all through the dough. Add enough flour to make dough soft and kneadable, but doesn't stick to your fingers. Let it rise again in a pan, then bake.]

This is how Jesus' words work in our lives. First, we listen to Jesus' words when we read the Bible. Before long, His words help change how we act. As we remember what Jesus says, we do more and more what He asks us to do. We say nicer things to people. We help more. That's how Jesus makes us good. Isn't He wonderful? ●

Theme: Heaven

#106

Buried Treasure

"The kingdom of heaven is like a treasure hidden in a field." Matthew 13:44, ICB.

Materials: *a metal box or a can with a lid, something special for "treasure," a spade, a place to bury the "treasure." [Bury the treasure before teaching this lesson.]*

Jesus told a story about a man who was plowing in someone else's field. He had probably been hired to plow the field so seeds could be planted. We're going to dig in this box, as the man dug in the field.

Suddenly the man hit something hard. It was treasure. [Help child find treasure.] He was so excited! But the treasure wasn't his— it was in someone else's field. So the man covered up the treasure. [Cover treasure.]

He ran home and gathered up everything he owned. He hurried to the market and sold it all. Then he took the money and bought the field. [Let your child pretend to buy the plot of ground.] Now the treasure was *his!* It was more than enough to make up for everything in his house that he had sold.

Jesus says that finding the kingdom of heaven is like finding a treasure in a field. God's kingdom is worth everything we have. What kinds of things might we need to get rid of so Jesus can live in our hearts? [Discuss.] ●

Theme: Treasure

The Best Pearl

"The kingdom of heaven is like a man looking for fine pearls."
Matthew 13:45, ICB.

Materials: *fake pearls, fake money, paper.*

J esus told another story about a merchant that was almost like the story of the buried treasure. People who own stores are merchants. They go shopping to buy things for their stores. Then they sell these things in their stores.

The merchant in Jesus' story was looking for fine pearls. Pearls are made by a certain kind of oyster. When a grain of sand gets in the oyster shell, it bothers the oyster, like getting sand in your shoes bothers you. The oyster makes a creamy liquid to cover the sand so it doesn't irritate it so much. This is the beginning of a pearl. As the oyster keeps covering the sand particle, the pearl gets bigger and bigger. People dive into the ocean to find the oysters that make pearls.

Jesus said the merchant once saw a pearl so beautiful that he wanted it more than all the other pearls in the world. So he sold everything he had to get enough money to buy that pearl.

Finding the kingdom of heaven is like finding the most special pearl in all the world. It is worth giving all that we have to get it.

[You can act out this story, or draw a picture of the oyster and the pearl.] ●

Theme: Treasure

#108

Honoring Our Family

"A prophet is honored everywhere except in his own town or in his own home."
Matthew 13:57, ICB.

Materials: *note-writing materials.*

Jesus was once invited to a town where the people didn't like Him. It was Jesus' hometown, Nazareth. It should have been the place people liked Him the best, but it wasn't.

As Jesus was teaching in the synagogue in Nazareth, people poked each other and whispered, "How did Jesus get to be so smart and be able to work miracles?" "We know him! His dad was a carpenter, right here in town!" "His mom is sitting right over there with his brothers and sisters."

And they turned against Jesus.

Jesus said to them, "A prophet from God is honored everywhere else except in his hometown and among his own family."

Sometimes we treat people we love worse than we do strangers. We tease our brothers and sisters, and act nicely to kids we don't even know. Of course, we should be nice to strangers. But we should be especially nice to our family. [Discuss why.]

Let's each think of something secret and special to do for each person in our family today—something helpful, or a little note or a picture to hide where they'll find it.

Theme: Family Love

Five Loaves and Two Fish

"Bring the bread and the fish to me."
Matthew 14:18, ICB.

Materials: *flour (whole-wheat is best), salt, oil, water. [Method: Stir a little salt into one cup of flour. Add enough water and a little oil to make a soft dough. Knead until smooth. Roll into thin circles. Bake on hot skillet, turning to brown both sides.]*

One day Jesus heard the sad, sad news that John the Baptist had been killed. He wanted to be alone with His friends so they could think about John the Baptist and how much they loved him. So Jesus got into a boat with His friends and went far away from the crowds and towns. But the people couldn't bear to be without Jesus. They walked all the way around the lake so they could be close to Him.

Jesus knew that these people loved Him. So He talked to them. He made sick people well. The day was almost over. It was almost suppertime, and because the people had walked a long way they were far from any village where they could buy food. They were hungry.

"Is there any food?" Jesus asked. Yes, there were five small loaves and two fish from a little boy's lunch.

That wasn't much. But Jesus would make a miracle. [With child, make the flatbread. This is similar to the loaves the boy had.] ●

Theme: Jesus' Care

#110

Jesus Makes a Miracle

"They all ate and were satisfied."
Matthew 14:20, NIV.

Materials: *Basket, bread, cheese (or vegetarian sandwich meat), water.*

Many, many people had followed Jesus around the lake. It was getting late in the day and they were hungry. But the only person who had food was a small boy. He had five little loaves of bread and two small fish.

"Bring the food to Me," Jesus replied. He said the blessing, broke the loaves, gave the food to His friends, and they gave it to the people. The bread and fish just kept growing and growing. The more Jesus broke off, the more there was. They all had a wonderful supper.

What a loving Jesus, to give a supper to all those tired, hungry people! And how kind of the boy to give away his picnic lunch so that Jesus could give everyone something to eat!

You can make a simple little picnic lunch like the boy shared with Jesus. Put five little pieces of bread in a basket. Cut two pieces of cheese or vegetarian sandwich meat into fish shapes. The boy might have found water in a spring, but you can take water in a jar.

Tell yourself some of Jesus' stories while you are eating, and listen for Jesus' voice as the Holy Spirit talks to you about Him in your heart. ●

Theme: Jesus' Care

Walking on the Water

"Have courage! It is I! Don't be afraid."
Matthew 14:27, ICB.

Materials: *toy boat, two doll figures (such as Ken dolls) for Peter and Jesus.*

esus needed to be alone, so He went off by Himself to pray. While He prayed, Jesus' friends were trying to row their boat across the lake. But the water was very rough. Jesus finished praying. He came down to the lake and walked across the water toward His friends. They were terrified to see a man walking on the water. "Don't be afraid," Jesus called. "It's just Me!"

Then Peter wanted to try walking on water too. He asked Jesus to tell him to come walk on the water. "Come," Jesus said.

So Peter climbed out of the boat and began walking toward Jesus. The wind was still blowing hard, and Peter became afraid and began to sink. Quickly Jesus reached out and caught him. Then both Jesus and Peter climbed into the boat, and the wind became still.

Act out this story with a little boat and doll figures. You can do it in the bathtub if you like. [Discuss.] Do you like to be alone sometimes? What do you do when you are alone? It's good to have a little time alone every day to pray, just as Jesus did. ●

Theme: Trust

#112

Doing What's Important

"Honor your father and mother."
Matthew 15:4, ICB.

Materials: *paper; pencils or crayons.*

The priests and teachers, who often made trouble for Jesus, came to see Him again. "Why don't your disciples wash their hands the right way?" they asked.

Jesus said, "What about you? Are you doing things the right way? The way you wash your hands is not important. But the way you treat people is very important. Do you treat your mother and father nicely? Do you treat My friends and Me nicely? No, you make trouble for us. You *say* you love God, but you don't love God with your heart."

Do you fuss about the way other people in our family do things? Do you complain about things that aren't very important? Do you sometimes forget important things, such as being kind to each other?

We'll put up two papers where we can see them. [Write "Important" on one paper; "Not Important" on the other.] When an argument comes up, we'll come to our papers and decide what is important. Then we can talk about how to solve our problems in a way that is kind to everyone. ●

#113

Theme: Family

A Woman of Faith

*"The woman . . . knelt before him. . . .
'Lord, help me!' she said."*
Matthew 15:25, NIV.

Jesus and His friends usually didn't go far from Galilee. But one day they took a trip to the ocean coast. A woman who had heard of Jesus lived there. Because she was from a different religion, Jesus' friends didn't want to have anything to do with her. They thought Jesus wouldn't want to, either. But that's one reason Jesus had made the long trip. He knew she needed His help. "Be kind to me," she cried out to Jesus. "Make my daughter well."

"Send her away," Jesus' friends said. "Listen to how she cries after us." The disciples still hadn't learned that Jesus loved everyone. Jesus loved people from countries and religions that were different from their own. Then Jesus said something strange. He was testing the woman and His friends. "I just came to help people who believe My religion," He said.

"Help me," she pleaded.

Jesus looked at her with love in His eyes. His disciples wondered what Jesus would do. What do you think Jesus did? Do you think He helped the woman? [Role-play Jesus and the woman who asked Him for help.] ●

Theme: Jesus' Love

#114

Children or Doggies?

"Woman, you have great faith! I will do what you asked me to do."
Matthew 15:28, ICB.

Materials: *globe or picture of the world; red, yellow, black, brown, white paper; glue.*

Yesterday we talked about a woman who asked Jesus to heal her daughter. "I'm not supposed to help people like you," Jesus replied. (Jesus meant that because she was from a different country, His friends expected Him to turn her away.) "You are like a puppy dog," Jesus said.

"If I'm like a doggie," she replied, "then you can give me a little help. Doggies eat crumbs from the children's table."

Jesus loved that answer! Of course He would help her! But He wanted to show His friends how much other people in the world needed His help. They were all His children.

"Oh, what great faith you have!" He told the woman. "I will heal your daughter."

Let's sing the song "Jesus loves the little children, all the children of the world."

Make a paper chain of the colors of the people around the world—black, brown, red, yellow, and white. Stretch it around a globe, or across a picture of the world. We are all part of Jesus' family. ●

15

Theme: Faith

Signs

"When you see the sunset, you know what the weather will be." Matthew 16:2, ICB.

Activity: *walk.*

Jesus climbed up a mountain and sat down, and thousands of people came to Him. Those who were sick, those who couldn't see or talk or walk—they all came to Him, and He healed them. He fed them all, just as He had done before.

But some still didn't want to accept Jesus as God's Son. "Give us a sign," they said.

"You can tell the weather from signs in the sky," Jesus said. "If the sky is red at night, you say it will be good weather. If the sky is red in the morning, you know it's going to storm. You're good at reading the weather signs. Why can't you read all the signs I'm giving you?"

Every good thing Jesus said and did was a sign that He was from God.

[Take a walk.] What signs can you read? Can you see signs of animals? What do they tell you? Can you see road signs? What about weather signs? Are there any signs of a new season, such as fall or spring coming? There are signs all over, telling us many things.

What signs show how the Holy Spirit is working in your heart? [Discuss.] ●

Theme: Holy Spirit

The Tough Times

"If anyone wants to follow me, he must say 'no' to the things he wants."
Matthew 16:24, ICB.

Materials: *11" x 14" piece of paper, scissors, marker. [Method: Make wide accordian-like folds in paper. Cut out a figure of a person, leaving hands and feet uncut on fold. Open up string of figures.]*

Jesus wanted His friends to think carefully about how they felt about Him. Sometimes it would be hard to be Jesus' friend. "It won't always be easy to be My friend," Jesus said, "because some people hate Me. They will hate you, too." Jesus wants everyone to be happy, but sometimes things in the world are sad. We must learn that God's way is always best, even though it isn't always fun at first.

Sometimes even our family has times that aren't fun. [Discuss. Sickness. When children disobey. Parents' jobs take too much time.] If we work hard at loving each other when it isn't easy, we'll have a stronger, happier family. [Discuss some strategies, i.e., family conferences, prayer, playing together.]

Take the "paper doll" figures you've cut out, and make into a circle. Fold each one's knees so family is "praying." Praying is one of the best ways to love each other through tough times. ●

#17

Theme: Family

Vision on the Mountain

"This is my Son and I love him. I am very pleased with him. Obey him!"
Matthew 17:5, ICB.

Activity: *listening game.*

P eter, James, and John went with Jesus to a high mountain. Jesus prayed, and the others fell asleep. Two special visitors came from heaven to see Jesus. One was Moses. Jesus had awakened him from death and taken him to heaven. The other was Elijah. He'd gone up to heaven in a fiery chariot. Moses and Elijah came to give Jesus courage for the time when He would die for our sins.

Peter and his friends woke up and saw that Jesus' face was shining like the sun, and His clothes were dazzling white. They heard a voice say, "This is my Son . . . listen to him" (Luke 9:35, REB).

Let's play a listening game. I'll ask you to do something, and you see how well you can listen and do it. I'll practice listening too. [Give one simple direction, such as "Sit on the floor." Let your child give you a direction. Next, give two directions: "Turn around three times and open the drapes." Alternate with child. Increase the number of directions and play as long as it's fun.] It's fun to listen carefully, isn't it? This is how we should listen to Jesus. ●

Theme: Listening

#118

MBFJ-17

Faith Like a Mustard Seed

"All things will be possible for you."
Matthew 17:20, ICB.

Activity: *role-play.*

As Jesus, Peter, James, and John were coming down from the mountain, they saw a crowd gathered around a sick boy. When the boy's father saw Jesus, he ran to Him and fell on his knees. "Have pity on my son," he pleaded. "Your disciples can't heal him." Jesus had given His friends power to heal in His name. But they had been quarreling. They were fighting about who was the best.

Jesus healed the boy. Later, when they were alone with Jesus, the disciples asked Him why they hadn't been able to heal the boy. "Your faith was too small," Jesus said. "Truly I tell you: if you have faith no bigger than a mustard seed, you will say to this mountain, 'Move from here to there!' and it will move; nothing will be impossible for you" (Matthew 17:20, REB).

It doesn't take much faith in God for Him to help you! Faith as tiny as a little seed is enough! But when we fight and argue, we don't have even that much faith. [Discuss things people quarrel about and what Jesus would do instead. Act out arguments and practice solving them in ways that would be good for everybody.] ●

#119

Theme: Faith

Fishing for Money

"Inside its mouth you will find a coin."
Matthew 17:27, ICB.

Activity: *Flatten one end of paper tube and tape shut. Make "mouth" by folding in two sides on other end of tube. Poke yarn or fishing line through one side of "mouth." Decorate with colored tissue. To use as a bank, put money in its mouth.*

oor Peter! The collectors of the Temple tax asked him a tricky question. "Does your master pay Temple tax?" they asked.

"He does," Peter said. Then Peter went to the house where Jesus and His friends were staying. Before Peter could say a word, Jesus asked him a question. He already knew about the question the Temple tax collectors had asked Peter.

Jesus said, "Who does a king make pay tribute to him?"

"Kings make conquered people pay tribute, but not their own people," Peter answered.

"That's right," Jesus said. "That's the reason we don't have to pay Temple tax. We're doing God's work, the same as the priests and teachers are doing. Those men want to trick us into paying the tax so it will look like we aren't doing God's work. But that's OK. We'll pay it anyway so that no one gets upset!" Then Jesus told Peter to go fishing! The first fish he caught would have in its mouth a coin to pay the Temple tax. How wise and kind Jesus was! [Follow directions above to make a fish bank.] ●

Theme: Money

#120

D
e
v
o
t
i
o
n

Who Is the Greatest?

"You must change and become like little children." Matthew 18:3, ICB.

Materials: *photos of child; favorite pictures from cards and magazines; 12" x 16" piece colored contact paper; 12" x 16" piece clear contact paper.*

Some of Jesus' friends were quarreling. "Who is the greatest person in the kingdom of heaven?" they asked Jesus.

Jesus called a little boy who was playing nearby. The little boy came running. "Do you see this little boy?" Jesus asked. "If you want to be great in My kingdom, you need to change and become simple and humble like this little child." And people who have the sweet, open, humble hearts, such as children have, are great too.

Isn't it wonderful that you don't have to do a lot of big important things for Jesus to think you're great? Jesus is so glad when you talk to Him and tell Him everything you are thinking and feeling. He made you special, just the way you are.

Make a Jesus-thinks-I'm-special place mat. Cut a piece of colored contact paper the size of a place mat (about 12" x 16"). Arrange some of your favorite pictures from cards and magazines on the sticky side of the contact paper. Add some photos and the words "Jesus thinks I'm special." Cover your pictures with clear contact paper. ●

Theme: Service

Angels Who Watch

"I tell you that they have angels in heaven who are always with my Father in heaven." Matthew 18:10, ICB.

Materials: *white paper, pencil, scissors, string, tape.*

Y ou are so important to Jesus that He said that if anyone hurt you or kept you from Him, "it would be better for him to have a millstone hung round his neck and be drowned in the depths of the sea" (Matthew 18:6, REB). A millstone is a huge stone that's used to grind flour. Jesus wants no one making trouble for you!

And Jesus added, "Be sure that you always treat little ones kindly and respectfully. Each one . . . has angels who watch over them, and the angels let My heavenly Father know how the little children are being cared for." You see how much Jesus loves you! You can't see your angels now. But they always take care of you.

Let's make some paper angels to hang over your bed and remind you that the angels watch over you. Fold a white sheet of paper in half, lengthwise. Lay your thumb along the fold. Have someone trace over the top of your thumb—the angel's head. Trace around your fingers for the angel's wings. Now take your hand away and draw the angel's gown. Cut it out and hang it over your bed. ●

Theme: Jesus' Love

#122

Your Brother and Sister

"If your brother sins against you, go and tell him what he did wrong."
Matthew 18:15, ICB.

Activity: *role-play, family puppets.*

esus knew that sometimes even brothers and sisters and friends hurt each other's feelings. Have you ever wondered what to do when you saw someone doing wrong? What did you do? [Discuss.] Jesus said, "If your brother does wrong, go and talk to him about it, just between yourselves." There is a good way to talk to people who are doing wrong:

1. Tell them what they are doing. You can say, "You are crashing my truck into the wall."

2. Tell them how you feel, and why. You might say, "I am worried, because I'm afraid you are going to break it."

3. Say what you want them to do. You can say, "Please play nicely with my truck."

Practice talking this way with your family. Use the following situations:

Your brother let the screen door slam in your face. Your sister is taking too long in the bathroom.

Your brother has left his coat on the floor in the living room. Your mom is yelling at you because she's tired. Your dad is being impatient about the traffic. ●

#123

Theme: Fixing Wrongs

Forgiving 490 Times

"I do not say to you, up to seven times, but up to seventy times seven."
Matthew 18:22, NASB.

Materials: *paper, marker. [After lesson, make 490 marks on the paper—70 times 7.]*

Do you remember how to talk to someone who is doing something wrong? [Review the three steps from yesterday's reading.] If your brother or sister or friend listens to you, you have won them over. But what if they don't? What if they keep doing wrong again and again?

Jesus says that next you should take one or two other people with you when you talk to that person. Is there something that keeps giving you problems? What person could you take with you to talk to the one who's doing wrong? [Discuss.]

Peter asked, "Jesus, how often should I forgive my brother if he keeps doing wrong? As many as seven times?"

Jesus said, "I do not say seven times. Do it seventy times seven."

Peter thought 70 times seven was a lot of times to forgive someone. It's almost too many to count. Seventy sevens is 490. Jesus meant that we should *always* forgive. That's what He does for us. ●

Theme: Forgiveness

#124

Showing Mercy

"So the master told the servant he did not have to pay." Matthew 18:27, ICB.

Activity: *role-play, family puppets.*

Jesus told this story to teach us about forgiveness. A servant owed a king so much money he could never pay it. "Sell this man as a slave," the king ordered.

The servant fell at the king's feet. "Be patient," he begged. "I will pay everything."

The king felt sorry for his servant, so he let him go. And he forgave his servant's debt. The servant left the palace a free man. He didn't owe the king a penny! Just then he met a man who owed him a few dollars. He grabbed the man and yelled "Pay me!"

"Be patient with me, and I will pay you," the man begged. But the servant had the man thrown into jail.

When the king heard about this, he was angry. "I forgave your huge debt, but you did not forgive a small debt!" he said, and put the man in jail.

Jesus told the people, "God has forgiven you for all the things you've done wrong. So you must forgive others."

[Act out this story. Role-play situations in which you need to forgive.] ●

Theme: Forgiveness

Let the Children Come

"Let the little children come to me."
Matthew 19:14, ICB.

Materials: *two paper plates, scissors, pen.*
[Method: On one plate, trace your
child's right hand, fingers close
together, thumb separate. Cut a
second hand, facing the opposite
way. Glue hands together, one hand
down and to the right of the other.]

The moms and dads wanted Jesus to put His hands on their children's heads and pray for them. So they brought their children to Jesus. But some people thought Jesus was too busy teaching grown-ups to bother with blessing children. They scolded the parents and tried to send the children away.

"No!" Jesus said, and called the children back. "Let the children come to me; do not try to stop them; for the kingdom of Heaven belongs to such as these" (Matthew 19:14,

REB). Jesus took the children on His lap and held them close. He put His hands on their heads and asked God to help them grow strong and be happy. He told them how much God loved them, and how glad He was that they had come to see Him.

"Do you see these children?" Jesus asked. "See how they listen to Me with all their hearts? They trust Me to take care of them. The kingdom of heaven belongs to people who love Me, as these children do."

Jesus will bless you, too, if you ask Him. He loves to be with you. [Make praying hands. Write your name on the cuff.] ●

Theme: Jesus, Our Friend

#12

"What Good Must I Do?"

"Give the money to the poor."
Matthew 19:21, ICB.

Activity: *trip to a new neighborhood.*

One day a young man asked Jesus a question: "What good do I have to do to live forever?"

We can never be *good* enough to go to heaven. But Jesus died for us so God could look at Jesus' clean, good life, instead of our lives. Jesus' goodness makes us good enough to go to heaven.

"Keep the commandments," Jesus told him. If Jesus is in our hearts, we will do what He wants us to.

"Oh, I have done that," the young man said. "Then sell everything you have and come follow Me." The young man looked very sad. He couldn't bear the thought of selling his beautiful things, even to follow Jesus. So he went away with a heavy heart. Jesus was sad too. He wanted the man to be His friend. But there were too many things the young man liked more than being with Jesus.

What kinds of things could keep you away from Jesus? ●

Theme: Money, use of

Following Jesus

"Come, follow me." Matthew 19:21, ICB.

Remember that yesterday we talked about a rich young man who said that he wanted to follow Jesus. But this man didn't want to give up any of his riches for Jesus.

Are there things that keep you from feeling close to Jesus? When we want our own way, we shut Jesus out of our hearts. How sad He feels then!

Jesus doesn't ask everyone to sell everything he or she has. Jesus is glad that you have toys to play with. But we should always be willing to give up anything for someone who might need it more.

Is there anyone you know who needs something you have? Do you have toys or clothes you can share? If you don't know anyone, maybe you should make some new friends in a part of town in which there are needs.

A good way to start doing this is to visit churches in neighborhoods that are poorer than yours. Make friends there. And pray that Jesus will help you find someone who needs you. What can you do today?

Theme: Sharing

#128

The Eye of a Needle

"This is something that men cannot do. But God can do all things."
Matthew 19:26, ICB.

Materials: *needle, thread, picture of a camel.*

Jesus sadly watched the rich young man walk away and said, "Truly I tell you . . . it is easier for a camel to pass through the eye of a needle than for a rich man to enter the kingdom of God" (Matthew 19:23, 24, REB). Here. Try to put the thread through the eye of this needle. Sometimes it's hard to do. Imagine putting a *camel* through that hole!

Jesus may have been talking about a small gate in the wall that was opened when the big gates were closed. Whether it was a sewing needle or a tiny gate, it would be impossible for a camel to fit. Jesus said it was easier for a camel to go through that small gate than for a rich man to be saved.

"Then who can be saved?" Jesus' friends asked.

Jesus looked at them and said, "For men this is impossible; but everything is possible for God" (verses 25, 26, REB).

No one can keep God's rules well enough to go to heaven. We can't be unselfish enough. We just can't be good enough! It's impossible! But God does the impossible. He saves us! Heaven is a wonderful free gift. What a great God to love and serve!

Theme: Salvation

Peter's Question

"He came to serve others."
Matthew 20:28, ICB.

Materials: *drawing paper, pencils.*

Have you noticed that some people talk more than others? Some children are quiet, and others are full of questions. What kind are you? Do you know anyone who is different from you? [Discuss.] We need all kinds of people in our world. Jesus' friend Peter asked a lot of questions. We've learned a lot from reading stories about what Peter said and did.

This time Peter wanted to know what was going to happen to him and his friends when Jesus set up His kingdom. "Well," Jesus answered, "you will each sit on a throne too. And if you have left houses or brothers or sisters or father or mother or children or land for My sake, you will be repaid many times over, and you will gain eternal life!"

Jesus is always fair, isn't He? If He asks us to give up something for His sake, He will always make it up to us. He will always give us much more than we ever gave Him.

Draw a picture of each member of your family. Beside each picture, write down how this person is different from the others. What special thing would you miss if they weren't around?

Theme: Loyalty

#130

Being Fair

"So those who have the last place now will have the first place in the future." Matthew 20:16, ICB.

Materials: *paper plate, paper fastener (or use clock from 103). [Make a paper clock. Move the hands to show how the clock shows the passage of time.]*

At 6:00 one morning a man hired some workers to weed his vineyard. At 9:00 the man found some more workers for his vineyard. "I will pay you a fair wage," he said. All day more workers came. Some didn't start work until 12:00 noon, and others began at 3:00. At 5:00 he sent another group of workers to work.

At 6:00 the sun went down, and it was time to pay everyone. And *everyone* got a full day's pay. Those who had worked all day were upset. "It isn't fair! Those who worked only an hour got the same pay as we did." [Help child count the hours.]

"I was fair to you," the man said. "I gave you the money we agreed I would pay you. Why are you complaining because I've paid the others more. It's my money, isn't it?"

Jesus is like the man who owned the vineyard. Have you ever thought that other children have better things than you have? [Discuss.] But Jesus gives all of us things that we need, and things we don't deserve. We don't need to worry about whether other people are getting more than we are. Jesus loves each one of us and gives us what we need. ●

Theme: Fairness

Time to Go to Jerusalem

"They will laugh at him . . . and then they will kill him on a cross."
Matthew 20:19, ICB.

Activity: *jumping.*

It was time for Jesus to go to Jerusalem. This is why He had come to the world. He would die so we could be saved. But His friends loved Him so much. [Discuss why.] He was a wonderful teacher and friend, and they didn't want Him to leave. They couldn't understand why He was going to be crucified. They wanted to be with Jesus forever.

Again and again Jesus tried to help them understand. What *God* knows is good is not always what looks good to *us.* "In Jerusalem," Jesus said, "they will condemn Me to death on the cross. But on the third day, I will be raised to life again."

And soon Jesus is coming to take all His friends who ever lived to heaven with Him.

Jump as high as you can. Now imagine a jump that takes you back to when God created the earth. Now imagine jumping all the way up to when Jesus died. Now jump up to where we are living now. The next jump will take you to the Second Coming. We can jump just a little, but God's "jumps" cover all time. And He is coming soon. ●

Theme: Salvation

#132

The Servant Leader

"If one of you wants to become great, then he must serve the rest of you like a servant." Matthew 20:26, ICB.

Materials: *apron or washcloth, towel, iron-on fabric, string, thread. [Use a store-bought apron or sew a washcloth to a hand towel. Add ribbon or string to tie it with. Iron on the letters for "Helper."]*

The mother of James and John came to see Jesus. She wanted to ask Him a favor. "What do you want?" He asked.

"Give orders that in Your kingdom my two sons can have a throne, one on Your left and one on Your right." She wanted her sons to have a better place than anyone else in Jesus' kingdom. Jesus knew that James and John loved Him. But they still didn't understand what His kingdom was about.

Jesus' other friends were angry. They thought they were just as important as James and John. What a mean trick to ask for special favors! So they started quarreling again. Do you ever quarrel because someone tries to get more than you have?

Jesus called His friends together. He told them that if they wanted to be great, they should be a servant. "I did not come to be served, but to serve, and to give My life to save yours," He said.

What kind of servant are you? Do you keep your eyes open to see where you can help? Are you happy when you are helping? ●

#133

Theme: Service

The Gentle King

"You will find a donkey tied there with its colt. Untie them and bring them to me." Matthew 21:2, ICB.

Materials: *cut branches or scarves, bandannas, sticks (Can use in 135.)*

Jesus and His friends were coming close to Jerusalem. Jesus sent two friends to a nearby village. "You will find a donkey and her baby [foal] tied up there," Jesus told them.

The disciples brought the donkey to Jesus. They laid their cloaks on the donkey, and Jesus climbed on its back. Crowds of people followed as Jesus rode slowly into the city.

Some people cut palms from nearby trees to spread on the ground. Everyone was wild with excitement. They were singing and shouting, "Hosanna to the Son of David! Blessed is he who comes in the name of the Lord! Hosanna in the heavens!" (Matthew 21:9, REB).

This was the way a king came into a city. What a glad day! Everyone was singing about Jesus! We can have a great time singing praise songs too, for Jesus is our king, and He is coming soon to take us to His kingdom. Cut some branches, or make some banners out of scarves or bandannas and a stick. Wave your branches or banners and sing some praise songs you know. "Praise Him, praise Him, all ye little children" is an old favorite. ●

Theme: Praise

MBFJ-19

#134

A House of Prayer

"My Temple will be a house where people will pray." Matthew 21:13, ICB.

Activity: *role-play.*

Remember how Jesus came riding a donkey into Jerusalem like a king? His next stop was the Temple. Boldly Jesus strode up the Temple steps. Oh, no. Inside the Temple were people buying and selling. Jesus knocked over the tables of the money changers. Coins flew everywhere! He knocked over the seats of the men who were selling pigeons. He told them all to get out, and they did.

Jesus said, "Scripture says, 'My house shall be called a house of prayer,' but you are making it a bandits' cave'" (Matthew 21:13, REB).

The men who were buying and selling things were not thinking about prayers or God. They were not helping the people come closer to God in their worship. Instead, they were cheating and stealing from the people who had come to worship.

How about you and me? Are Sabbath and church always a blessing? Let's act out some of the things that happen on Sabbath. [Start with getting ready for church. Experiment with ideas that would make church a more prayerful, positive experience.] ●

35

Theme: God's House

Hosanna, Again!

The children were saying, "Praise to the Son of David." Matthew 21:15, ICB.

Activity: *singing.*

Materials: *branches or bandannas.*

After the shopkeepers were gone, Jesus sat down with the people who loved to be near Him. [Who were they? Discuss.] Now the Temple felt like a good place to be, because Jesus was there. The children had had such an exciting day that they began to sing the hosanna song again. "Hosanna to the Son of David! Hosanna, Hosanna!" they shouted.

The priests and teachers were angry to hear the singing. "Do you hear those children? Stop them!"

"I hear them," Jesus said. "Haven't you read where God tells the children and babies to sing praise out loud? I won't stop them."

Even little children can listen to God speaking in their hearts. These children were so happy they couldn't help singing. God wants us all to be happy, and to tell others why we love Jesus so much. Sing some of your favorite praise songs. Think who might like to hear your songs. Take your banners or branches along and sing for your grandparents, neighbors, or friends at church, or in a nursing home. Jesus loves to hear you sing! ●

Theme: Obedience

 #13

The Withered Tree

"How did the fig tree dry up so quickly?"
Matthew 21:20, ICB.

Activity: *Break off a stem of a plant several
hours before lesson time to observe
withering process.*

Jesus was hungry and saw a fig tree
by the road. It was full of leaves, so
there should have been figs on it
too. But there weren't any. "He said to the
tree, 'May you never bear fruit again!' and
at once the tree withered away" (Matthew
21:19, REB).

Jesus' friends were shocked. Why would
He kill a tree? But the wilted tree was a lesson to all who didn't love and obey God.
These people sounded like they had the good
fruit of love. But they didn't. So Jesus showed
what would happen to people like that.

Our loving, kind Jesus is also fair. He
may wait a long time, trying to help those
who hate Him to change their ways. But
He won't wait forever. Look at this withered piece of plant. What has happened to
the leaves? Why? What keeps the leaves
healthy when they are on the plant? How
can *we* keep from withering? How can we
be a tree full of good fruit when Jesus
comes to us?

We need to stay close to God. He
makes us strong. Singing happy songs
about Jesus is one good fruit we can give
Him. Can you think of others? ●

137

Theme: Fairness

Throwing Mountains Into the Sea

"And if you have faith, it will happen."
Matthew 21:21, ICB.

Materials: *paper.*

One day Jesus was talking to His friends about prayer. He told them that they should pray for big things as well as little things. "Whatever you pray for in faith," Jesus said, "you will receive."

Faith! That's all we need. Faith in God's power to help us. Faith that God's ways are right. When we pray to Him, we can remind Him of His promises to help us. And we must pray that His way—not our way—be done. Our ideas of God are too small. He is much greater, much more powerful, and much more willing to help us than we can imagine.

Is there something that you need God to help you do? Does it seem so impossible it's like making a mountain jump into the sea? Are you willing that God answer your prayer in the way He knows is best?

Draw a picture of what you're praying for. Put down today's date. Every day that you pray about this, write the date on the picture, and what God has done so far. God is willing to move mountains for you. [Discuss what "moving mountains" means.] •

Theme: Faith

#138

Who's Your Boss?

"Tell us! What authority do you have to do these things?" Matthew 21:23, ICB.

Materials: *two socks; button eyes; red felt for mouth; yarn, rags, or netting for hair. [Method: To make puppet, cut slits in the toe end of each sock; sew on a red, oval mouth. Sew on button eyes and "hair."]*

Jesus was teaching in the Temple when some priests and teachers came over to listen. They just wouldn't leave Jesus alone. "Who told you that you could teach here in the Temple? Who's your boss, anyway?" they asked.

Jesus asked them a question. "Who told John the Baptist to preach? God, or men?"

The men said to each other, "If we say God sent him, Jesus will ask why we didn't believe him. But if we say he was from men, the people will be angry, because they believe he was from God." So they told Jesus,

"We don't know."

Of course, they already knew that Jesus had come from God too. But they just wanted to argue with Jesus, and He wouldn't argue with them.

How can you tell that somebody just wants to argue? [Discuss.] Maybe your brother is angry at someone else, but picks a fight with you. Sometimes we should just be quiet and walk away. Sometimes kindness works. [Let your puppets argue, and then help them figure out how to stop arguing.] ●

#139

Theme: Arguing

The Story of Two Boys

"Son, go and work today in my vineyard."
Matthew 21:28, ICB.

Activity: *role-play.*

Jesus didn't argue with the priests and teachers, but He did tell them a story:

A man had two sons. He asked one boy to work in the vineyard. "I will, sir," the boy said, but he didn't go. Maybe some neighbor boys came over to play.

So the father asked his other son to work in the vineyard. "I will not," the other boy said. But later he changed his mind. Maybe he was sorry for being rude. In any case, off he went to the vineyard to work.

"Which of the two boys did what his father wanted?" Jesus asked.

"The boy who worked," the priests and teachers answered.

Then Jesus said, "The people who you think are so bad will be saved before *you.* They are sorry for what they have done wrong, and they want to do what is right."

There weren't three boys in this story, but we can add a third boy who says "Yes, Father!" and goes and does what his father asks.

Role-play how you would answer your dad or mom.

Theme: Obedience

#140

The Story of the Vineyard

"There was a man who owned a vineyard." Matthew 21:33, ICB.

Materials: *green, purple, and white paper, and glue. [Method: Make a cluster of grapes from circles of purple paper. On each grape write a "fruit," such as "praise" or "love" that you want to give to Jesus. Glue grapes to paper; add a green grape leaf.]*

Jesus told another story about a vineyard. Once a man planted a vineyard. This man hired men to take care of all the grapevines, and then he took a trip. After the grapes were harvested, the owner sent his servants to collect money from the men taking care of the vineyard.

But the men in the vineyard beat and killed the servants. So he sent more servants. They were killed too. Finally the owner sent his son. "They will not hurt my *son,*" he said.

But the wicked men said, "Look, here is the man who will inherit this vineyard from his dad. Let's kill him, and we will own it!" So they did.

Jesus looked at the priests and teachers. *They* were the wicked men in God's vineyard. They had killed the prophets God sent to help the people, and were planning to kill Jesus, too.

You can give good "fruit" to Jesus by living His way. What kinds of "fruit" can you give to Jesus? [Make grape cluster as directed above.] ●

#141

Theme: Obedience

The Wedding Feast

"Yes, many people are invited. But only a few are chosen." Matthew 22:14, ICB.

Materials: *blank cards and envelopes.*

Jesus told another story about His kingdom: Once a king gave a party for his son's wedding. He sent his servants to call the guests, but the guests wouldn't come. So the king sent more servants, telling them to say, "I have the best food all ready for you. Come to the wedding party!" But one guest went off to his farm, another went off to his work, and the rest attacked the king's servants.

The king was furious. "We still are going to have the wedding party, but my first guests don't deserve to come. Go out into the streets, wherever you can find people, good or bad, and bring them to the party." So that's what the servants did. They collected everyone they could find, and the king's party was packed with guests.

Have you ever had a party invitation? God is the king, and He's inviting you to His party in heaven. Do you want to go? You can make an invitation to God's party in heaven. Be sure to tell "who, what, where, and when." Then write a letter back to God, letting Him know you want to come. I want to attend, don't you? ●

Theme: God's Party

MBFJ-20

#142

Wedding Clothes

"Yes, many people are invited. But only a few are chosen." Matthew 22:14, ICB.

Materials: *party materials for everyone, such as balloons, hats, decorated table, white T-shirts.*

The story of the wedding party wasn't over yet. Jesus said that the king came in to the party. He was glad that the guests were having fun. The food was delicious, and people were laughing and visiting. But one man wasn't dressed for a wedding. The king had given everyone beautiful clothes to wear to the party, but this man hadn't put his on. "My friend," the king said, "why aren't you wearing the wedding clothes?"

The man just shrugged. He just hadn't wanted to wear the clothes.

"Throw him out," the king said.

At God's party in heaven we'll wear special robes that Jesus gives us. It is His robe of goodness. Isn't it wonderful that Jesus gives us His beautiful robe to wear? And wouldn't it be a shame if we didn't want His goodness? I want to wear Jesus' white robe to His party in heaven.

Let's have a little party here to celebrate the big party in heaven. Let's put on our white "robes" and thank God for loving us so much that He gives us all the clothes we need to go to heaven. ●

#143

Theme: Salvation

Caesar's Coin

"Give to Caesar the things that are Caesar's." Matthew 22:21, ICB.

Materials: *coins, crayons or colored pencils, typing paper.*

One day the priests and teachers tried to trap Jesus in an argument. They brought along some of the king's men to help them. "We know you are an honest teacher," they said to Jesus. "So tell us, should we pay taxes to the Roman emperor?" Jesus saw the trap. If He said yes, the people would be angry because they hated the ruler who made them pay taxes. If He said no, the king's men would put Him in jail.

"You are trying to trick Me," Jesus said. "Whose picture is on the coin used to pay taxes?"

"Caesar's, the Roman emperor," they said.

"Then pay to Caesar what belongs to Caesar, and to God what belongs to God" (Matthew 22:21, REB).

Nobody knew what to say. So they went away and left Jesus alone. Wise, wise Jesus. We can always trust Him to know what is best! [Look at coins. Discuss faces and symbols.] We can make prints of these pictures on the coins by putting paper over the coins and coloring over them. Let's put these coins in the offering this Sabbath. ●

Theme: Money

#144

The Greatest Commandment

"Love the Lord your God with all your heart, soul and mind." Matthew 22:37, ICB.

Materials: *white paper, scissors. [Method: Fold paper in half and, with scissors, round the top. Leave bottom square. Open the tablet.]*

The priests and teachers were still trying to trap Jesus. "Teacher," they asked, "which is the greatest commandment?" (Matthew 22:36, REB). But whichever one of the Ten Commandments Jesus picked, they would argue about the nine He didn't pick. The first four commandments tell us how to worship God:

1. Don't put any other god before God.
2. Don't worship an idol as a god.
3. Don't use God's name in a wrong way.
4. Worship God as the Creator on the Sabbath.

Jesus turned these four commandments into one easy rule: Love God more than anything else! "That is the greatest, the first commandment" (verse 37, REB), He told them.

Well, nobody could argue with that.

Open your paper Ten Commandments. On the left side write "Love God." We'll write the second commandment later on during a worship. ●

Theme: Ten Commandments

The Second Commandment

"Love your neighbor as you love yourself."
Matthew 22:39, ICB.

Activity: *role-play ways of keeping these commandments.*

Jesus said the first commandment was to love the Lord with all your heart. When you think of God when you first get up, when you talk to Him during the day, and pray before you go to bed, you are putting God first. The second commandment, Jesus said, is like the first: "Love your neighbour as yourself" (Matthew 22:39, REB). God loves us all so much that He wants us to take good care of each other.

The last six commandments are about the way we should treat others:

5. Respect your parents.

6. Don't kill each other.
7. Don't take away someone else's husband or wife.
8. Don't steal.
9. Don't lie.
10. Don't wish you could have anything that belongs to someone else.

Role-play ways we keep these commandments. For example, not fighting or lying. ●

Theme: Ten Commandments ✂

#14

Loving Others as Yourself

"Love your neighbor as you love yourself."
Matthew 22:39, ICB.

Materials: *yellow paper, scissors, glue, "tablet" from lesson before last.*

Review last six commandments.] If you love others, you'll treat them as Jesus said to. You'll always be kind and respectful. You will share instead of grabbing things from others. You'll treat yourself well too, because you are important. You'll eat well and get lots of rest and exercise, because you'll remember that God loves you and wants you to take good care of yourself.

What if our world was full of people who loved God, their neighbors, and themselves? What a happy place this would be! We wouldn't need any police or soldiers or judges or jails. That's all the law is about—love!

On the second half of your commandment tablet write "Love your neighbor as yourself." Then cut out a big yellow sun with a happy face and glue the bottom part of the sun behind the commandment tablet. The sun can symbolize the glory and happiness we'll have when Jesus comes and all of us will keep God's laws in our hearts by loving each other. ●

Theme: Loving

What They Say and What They Do

"How terrible for you, teachers of the law and Pharisees! You guide the people, but you are blind." Matthew 23:16, ICB.

Activity: *doing things secretly to help others.*

It was sad, but many of the priests and teachers did not really love God. They were important leaders, and after Jesus went back to heaven they'd still be leading the people. So Jesus told the people what they were really like. "Respect these men, but don't do what they do. They like to dress up and look important, but they don't help people. They make big burdens for others that make their lives hard."

Jesus could see what people's hearts were like. And He knew these priests and teachers didn't love God or their neighbors.

If they did, they would want to make their lives easier.

Whose life can you make easier today? What can you do for your mom or dad or brother or sister? What about your neighbors and friends?

Plan something as a secret surprise! Just for fun, every time you do something special for someone, leave your "mark." You might leave a leaf or a button every time. Or you could leave a piece of paper stamped with a special stamp. Pick one thing as a secret identifier and have fun! ●

Theme: Service

#148

Humble Yourself

"Whoever makes himself humble will be made great." Matthew 23:12, ICB.

Materials: *red felt, safety pin, fabric marker. [Method: Cut a heart out of red felt. With marker, write "Heart of a servant" on it.]*

Jesus wanted to help the people know what a good leader was like, how they should treat a leader, and how to be a good leader.

"Don't make your priests and teachers more important than they are," Jesus said. "You have one Teacher, the Messiah. If you want to be great, be a servant. If you don't push yourself up and act as if you are important, people will respect you more."

Because of Jesus' instruction, Adventists don't call their ministers "Father" or "Reverend," for God is our Father.

Jesus said that we should humble ourselves. How do we do that? [Discuss.] What about at the dinner table? Do you let someone else get the first serving or the biggest piece of pie? Do you let others talk first? Being humble means not minding when others get ahead of us in line, or get more important jobs. We should be happy when someone else has nice things, even nicer than ours.

Pin the red heart to your clothes to help remind you that a "servant heart" is the best kind to have. ●

Theme: Service

Too Bad for You

"But you don't obey the really important teachings of the law—being fair, showing mercy, and being loyal." Matthew 23:23, ICB.

Activities: *discuss meaning of "hypocrite"; make list of values.*

Jesus had strong words for hypocrites that He knew. "You pay tithe on everything—even the herbs you grow in your window garden." ("One, two, three, four, five, six, seven, eight, nine mint leaves for me—one leaf for God.")

"But you don't care about loving people, being thoughtful and kind, making sure people are treated fairly. It's great to be careful about the little leaves in your window garden, but not if you forget the big, important things like being kind and loving and fair!"

Jesus knows all about us, doesn't He?

He knows if we make a big fuss about "little things" and forget the most important things. [Discuss.]

Draw a small circle at the top of one side of your paper and a big circle at the top of the other side. [Discuss what is most important in your family.] List these on the "big circle" side. [Discuss not-so-important things.] List these on the "small circle" side. [If children can't yet read, draw pictures about each of the items.] Post your list to help you remember your decisions about your values. ●

Theme: Kindness

#150

A Clean Cup

"You wash the outside of your cups and dishes." Matthew 23:25, ICB.

Activity: *dishwashing. Do lesson after you've washed dishes—washing outside, but leaving inside dirty. Ask child to rinse and dry. Discuss this [bad] method. Allow dishes to soak and move into lesson.*

Jesus made a word picture about people who looked good on the outside, but weren't good on the inside. First He talked about a cup. "You clean the outside of a cup or a dish, and leave the inside full of greed. . . . Clean the inside of the cup first; then the outside will be clean also" (Matthew 23:25, 26, REB).

We know all about cleaning dishes, don't we? The inside of the cup gets the dirtiest and needs the most cleaning! That's what Jesus says about our hearts. Our hearts need cleaning more than the outside of our bodies.

But Jesus will clean our hearts. Sometimes we have greed in our hearts. We are greedy when we want more than our share. Jesus will fill our hearts with love so that we are glad to give to other people. We will think more about others than ourselves.

Let's wash the inside of our dishes now. While we are washing, we can ask God to clean the insides of our hearts! ●

Theme: Salvation

A Mother Hen

"I wanted to gather them together as a hen gathers her chicks under her wings." Matthew 23:37, ICB.

Materials: *blanket.*

he last few days we've been talking about how Jesus sometimes scolded the people. But if you had been there to hear Him, you would have heard tears in His voice. Jesus was crying about what would happen to them after He died.

"O Jerusalem, Jerusalem, city that murders the prophets and stones the messengers sent to her!" Jesus said. "How often have I longed to gather your children, as a hen gathers her brood under her wings; but you would not let me" (Matthew 23:37, REB).

I'll show you how a mother hen covers her chickens. Let's pretend I'm the mother hen, and this blanket is my wings. [Cover your shoulders with the blanket; fold it over your arms, and wrap your child close to you within the blanket.] This is how Jesus wanted to take care of the children in Jerusalem. He wanted to protect them and keep them from the dangers that were coming.

I want to stay under Jesus' blanket, don't you? When Jesus comes again, we will be among the ones who go to live with Him. ●

Theme: God's Care

#152

Signs of Jesus' Coming

"The Good News about God's kingdom will be preached in all the world, to every nation. Then the end will come." Matthew 24:14, ICB.

Materials: *Sabbath school quarterlies with mission reports, savings bank.*

Jesus' friends worshipped in a beautiful Temple. It was made of white marble and gleamed in the sun like a snow castle. But Jesus told them that someday their Temple would be torn down. "When will all this happen?" they asked. "And how will we know when You're coming again?"

Jesus said that there would be wars and earthquakes, and that some people would hate those who love Him. These are all signs of the end. Then Jesus said something very special. "Everyone all over the world will hear the stories I have told you about the kingdom of God. Then the end will come." Before Jesus comes everyone will have a chance to know Him and to decide if they want to follow Him. That's why we read Jesus' stories. That's why missionaries go all over the world to tell everyone about Jesus.

What are you doing to tell others about Jesus? You are a missionary too! And you can help missionaries in their work. Look on the back page of our Sabbath school quarterly. Let's choose a project and save an offering for it. ●

#153

Theme: Second Coming

Like Lightning

"It will be like lightning flashing in the sky that can be seen everywhere."
Matthew 24:27, ICB.

Materials: *large sheets of paper (or an old sheet) for mural, sponge, paint. (Can also use in 180.)*

Activities: *trumpet playing, watching thunderstorm.*

esus warned His friends that before He came back, bad people would pretend to be Him. He told them not to believe them. "If someone says 'Look! Jesus is out in the desert,' don't believe it," He said. "It won't be Me. When I come with all the angels, everyone will see Me. The sky will be so bright that it will look like lightning flashing from east to west."

Jesus said that He would come in the clouds of heaven with power and great glory. "I will blow a loud blast on My trumpet; and My angels will gather everyone who loves Me from the four winds." Everyone can see lightning flash across all the sky. And Jesus' trumpet will be so loud that even the dead will hear it—and wake up! What a wonderful, happy, exciting day.

Make a mural of Jesus' coming. You can paint big, beautiful clouds. Make an angel stamp out of a piece of sponge so you can paint many angels quickly. And don't forget Jesus' trumpet! [If you have a trumpet, listen to its blasts and imagine Jesus calling us to be with Him. Watching a thunderstorm would be a great activity too.] ●

Theme: Second Coming ✏️ ❀

#154

Keep Awake! Stay Ready!

"So always be ready." Matthew 24:42, ICB.

Activity: *race. Before beginning, figure out where your start and finish lines will be.*

Let's have a little race, OK? Now, everybody get on our starting line. Get ready; get set; go! [Let your child race several times.] Show me how you felt when I said "Get ready."

These are important times. Jesus says, "Keep awake! Don't get drowsy and forget to watch for My coming!" Of course, Jesus didn't mean we shouldn't sleep. We need sleep to grow and stay healthy and strong. But He didn't want us to get tired of waiting for Him.

Pretend your dad was going on a trip and asked you to feed and give water to your dog while he was gone. What if Dad came back early and found the dog dish empty and the water dish dry? Would you say, "Oh, but Dad, I didn't know you were coming today! If I had known, I would have taken care of the dog!"

Dad would probably say, "You should *always* make sure the dog is taken care of. Then you would always be ready for me to come!"

Jesus wants us always to be ready for Him to come. "Be ready," He says, "because I will come when you don't expect Me." ●

Theme: Second Coming

A Story About 10 Girls

"So always be ready. You don't know the day or the time the Son of Man will come." Matthew 25:13, ICB.

Materials: *oil lamp, oil for lamp.*

Ten girls were waiting for the bridegroom to come to his wedding feast. Five girls were wise and took extra oil to burn in their lamps. The other five were foolish; if the bridegroom was late, they wouldn't have any extra oil. The bridegroom took a long time to come. The girls fell asleep, and their lamps burned lower and lower. Suddenly someone shouted, "Here comes the bridegroom!" The girls awoke with a start. Their lamps were going out, so the five girls with extra oil filled their lamps.

The foolish girls cried, "Oh, no! Can we borrow some of your oil?" But the wise girls said no. There wasn't enough extra oil for all 10 lamps. So the foolish girls ran to find more oil, and the wise girls went into the wedding feast. The door was shut. The foolish girls were too late to go to the feast.

In this story Jesus is the bridegroom. "Keep awake then," Jesus said, "because you don't know the day or the hour I will be coming."

[If you have an oil lamp, light it. Sing "This Little Light of Mine."] ●

Theme: Second Coming

#15

Our Bags of Gold

"You did well with small things. So I will let you care for much greater things."
Matthew 25:21, ICB.

Materials: *notebook.*

A man was leaving on a trip, Jesus said, so he gave his money to his servants to take care of. Five bags of gold went to one servant, two bags to another, and one bag to another.

The first servant used the gold to earn more gold. Maybe he bought wheat, ground it, and made bread to sell. When his master came back, he had 10 bags of gold to give him. The man with two bags of gold had worked hard, too. He had four bags of gold for his master. The master was very happy. "I see I can trust you to take care of small things," he said. "I will put you in charge of something big!"

But the man who'd been given one bag of gold was lazy. He'd buried it in the ground. His master was very angry and threw the useless servant out.

Jesus has given each of us special treasures too. Each of us are good at doing something. What special gifts do we have? [Discuss each person's gifts.] When we invest our gifts, they grow. How can you invest your gifts for Jesus? Let's write down our investment plan in a "Family Investment" notebook. ●

57

Theme: Talents

The Sheep and the Goats

"The Son of Man will come again in his great glory." Matthew 25:31, ICB.

Activity: *role-play, family puppets.*

W hen I come again," Jesus said, "I will come with all My angels. All the . . . people will gather around Me, and I will separate them into two groups.

"'You have My Father's blessing,' I will say to the group on My right. 'Come, take the kingdom I have made ready for you . . . For when I was hungry, you gave Me food; when I was thirsty, you gave Me something to drink; when I was a stranger, you took Me into your home . . . when I was ill, you came to help Me; when I was in prison, you visited Me.'

"These good people will say to Me, 'Jesus, when did we ever see You hungry or thirsty or a stranger . . . or sick or in prison?' And I will tell them, 'Whatever you did for the poorest . . . you did for Me.'"

It's very important to Jesus that we take care of each other. His angels keep a record of every good thing we do for someone else, or any good thing we fail to do.

Let's pretend you are playing with someone, but it is really Jesus. How would you play? [Role-play several situations with family and strangers.] ●

Theme: Kindness

#158

MBFJ-22

Washing Feet

"I, your Lord and Teacher, have washed your feet. So you also should wash each other's feet." John 13:14, ICB.

Materials: *basin, towel.*

It was the last time Jesus was going to eat supper with His 12 friends. They fixed the supper at a man's house in the city, and they all came together to eat it. Usually a servant washed their dusty feet before they ate, but all the servants were busy. The men looked at each other. No one wanted to act like a servant and wash the others' feet.

Quietly Jesus got up, poured water into a basin, and knelt before His friends to wash their feet. Now the men were sorry they had been so proud. When Jesus had finished, He told His friends, "If I, your Lord and Teacher, have washed your feet, you also ought to wash one another's feet" (John 13:14, REB).

That's why we wash each other's feet before we eat the Lord's Supper at church. We make sure we have no bad feelings about each other. We forgive each other, and serve each other by washing one another's feet.

We can wash each other's feet right here at home. First, we need to make sure we don't have any bad feelings. [Discuss.] Then we can wash each other's feet. ●

59

Theme: Forgiveness

The Passover

For God loved the world so much that he gave his only Son. God gave his Son so that whoever believes in him may not be lost, but have eternal life. John 3:16, ICB.

Materials: *gift box, wrapping paper, ribbon, small lamb, sticks, picture of Jesus, etc.*

In yesterday's story Jesus and His friends were eating the Passover supper. The children of Israel had eaten the very first Passover meal the night they had left Egypt. They'd eaten unleavened bread, bitter herbs, and Passover lamb. They had spread the lamb's blood on their doorposts, showing their faith in God's saving power. Every year since that time, the children of Israel had eaten the Passover meal and had killed the Passover lamb.

Now it was time for the true Lamb, Jesus, to die for the world. Jesus was like the pure little lamb. He hadn't done anything wrong. We have done wrong, of course. But instead of our dying for our sins, Jesus died instead. Jesus gave us His right to have life. What a wonderful present! Jesus' love makes us feel so good we want to sing! What do you feel like singing? [Sing some of your child's favorite songs.]

Let's wrap an open box to remind us of God's love. This shows that Jesus' gift is open and free for everyone to take. Let's put some things in the box to remind us of God's love. ●

Theme: Jesus' Death

#160

The Last Supper

"I will not drink of this fruit of the vine again until that day when I drink it new with you in my Father's kingdom."
Matthew 26:29, ICB.

Materials: *crackers, grape juice.*

As they had the Passover supper for the last time, Jesus told His friends, "I won't eat this again till we all eat together in My kingdom." Jesus picked up the bread, blessed it, and broke it into pieces. Giving it to His friends, He said, "Take this and eat; this is my body" (Matthew 26:26, REB). When we accept and eat the unleavened bread, we accept Jesus' gift to save us. Then Jesus took a cup of grape juice. He thanked God for it, then He gave it to His friends, saying, "Drink from it, all of you" (verse 27, REB). The grape juice was His promise that His blood would save us from our sins.

Sometimes we have the Lord's Supper at church. We wash each other's feet and eat the bread and drink the grape juice together. We think of Jesus' death for us and His promise to eat this supper with us when He takes us to heaven.

[You can have the Lord's Supper at home. Decorate the table and use candles. Start and end your supper with singing. Talk about your favorite stories of Jesus and what you'll do with Jesus when you see Him.] ●

#161

Theme: Last Supper

In the Garden

"Stay awake and pray for strength against temptation." Matthew 26:41, ICB.

Activity: *doing special things.*

After supper Jesus and His friends went to a garden where they often spent the night. But Jesus didn't sleep. His friends slept, but if they had known how hard the next day would be, they would have spent the night praying with Jesus. "My heart is ready to break," Jesus told them. "Stay awake with me" (Matthew 26:38, REB). Jesus went a little way from them and fell on His face in prayer.

This was a terrible night. Jesus had done nothing wrong, but He felt all the guilt of this wicked old world. He begged God, "Please tell Me I don't have to do this. But I will do whatever You wish." Jesus came back and found His friends sleeping. "Couldn't you stay awake with Me?" He asked. He went away and prayed again. "Father, Your will be done." Jesus worried that the sins He was suffering for would keep Him from seeing His Father again. But He would do it. He would do whatever His Father said.

[Do something special today to thank Jesus for dying for us. Remember, what you do for others, you do for Jesus.] ●

Theme: Jesus' Death

#162

Jesus Is Betrayed

"You are still sleeping and resting? The time has come for the Son of Man to be given to sinful people."
Matthew 26:45, ICB.

Activity: *role-play.*

The disciples were still sleeping when Jesus came back. "The hour has come!" He said. "I am given over to the hands of sinners." The disciples jumped up as rough men with swords and sticks surrounded them. Peter grabbed his sword and cut off one man's ear. But Jesus healed the man's ear and told Peter, "Put away your sword. If I wanted to, I could ask My Father to send thousands of angels to help Me."

Jesus looked sadly at the crowd. "Am I a robber that you come to catch Me at night?

But this is what the Scriptures say must happen." The disciples were scared. Why didn't Jesus get away? So *they* ran away and left Jesus with the bad men who hurried Him off to the priests and teachers.

The disciples had been friends of Jesus for a long time. But when Jesus needed them the most, they slept. And when the rough men grabbed Him, they ran away.

How should friends act? [Discuss.] What kind of friend are you?

Act out this scene of Jesus in the garden, being a good friend to Him. ●

#103

Theme: Jesus' Death

Jesus in the Priest's Court

"Tell us, are you the Christ, the Son of God?" Matthew 26:63, ICB.

Materials: *Ken dolls, shoe boxes, blocks.*

Activity: *set up city of Jerusalem; using dolls, reenact closing scenes of Jesus' life.*

ven though Peter and John had run away in fear, they wanted to know what happened to Jesus. So they followed the crowd to Caiaphas, the high priest. Those who always tried to make trouble for Jesus were there. Many told lies about Him, but their false stories didn't agree. The high priest asked Jesus, "Don't you have an answer to all these stories about you?" But Jesus didn't say a word.

The priest said, "I charge you, by the living God, to tell us. Are you the Son of God?"

"Yes," Jesus said. "The next time you see Me I will be sitting on the right hand of God, coming in the clouds of heaven."

"He's saying he is God!" the priest cried. "He should die."

And then they spat in His face and beat Him with their fists and said, "If you are a prophet, tell us who hit you." But Jesus didn't say a word. He was as quiet as a lamb.

[Set up a semi-permanent scene where you can help your child reenact the closing scenes of Jesus' life—riding on the donkey into Jerusalem; cleansing of the Temple, etc.] ●

Theme: Jesus' Death

#164

Devotion

Peter and the Rooster

"We know you are one of those men who follow Jesus. We know this because of the way you talk." Matthew 26:73, ICB.

Materials: *fire, rooster.*

Activity: *Make a little courtyard and fire from orange paper. Act out Peter's story.*

While Jesus was inside, Peter was out in the courtyard. Peter and others were around a fire, getting warm. A maid saw Peter. "I've seen you before," she said. "You were with Jesus."

Oh, no! Peter thought. *They'll arrest me, too!* So he said, "No, I don't know Him."

A little later a man asked, "Hey, you are one of Jesus' followers!" Peter said no.

"I know you were with Jesus. You are a Galilean," someone else said.

Peter got angry and used bad words. "I don't know what you are talking about," he shouted. Just then a rooster crowed. Suddenly Peter remembered that Jesus had told him, "Before the cock crows, you will deny Me three times."

Just then Jesus came out of the council room, pale and tired. He looked sadly at Peter. Peter's heart broke. How could he have lied that he didn't know Jesus, when Jesus had been so good to him? Peter ran back to the garden where Jesus had prayed and cried and cried. He felt so badly about how he had treated Jesus. Do we ever treat Jesus this way? [Discuss.] ●

#165

Theme: Jesus' Death

Judas

So Judas threw the money into the Temple. Matthew 27:5, ICB.

Materials: *30 pieces of silver (nickels, dimes, quarters).*

Judas had been one of Jesus' good friends, and he was smart. The other disciples were proud he was with them. But Judas was not happy with Jesus. Judas wanted to force Jesus to be a king right away. He didn't want to wait for Jesus to do things God's way. So Judas had gone to the priests and teachers. "What will you give me to tell you where Jesus is?" he had asked.

They gave him 30 pieces of silver. [Count out 30 pieces of money.] Then Judas showed them where Jesus was. But now Judas was even more upset. He'd thought Jesus would free Himself and make Himself king. Instead, Jesus didn't even try to get away.

Judas felt terribly guilty. "Here, take back your money!" he cried to the priests. "Jesus isn't a bad man! He shouldn't die!" But the priests didn't care. In anguish, Judas threw the 30 pieces of silver on the Temple floor and ran out.

But Judas still didn't soften his heart. He wasn't willing to do things God's way. When do we need to humble ourselves and listen? [Discuss.] ●

Theme: Jesus' Death

#16

Before Pilate

Jesus said, "My kingdom does not belong to this world." John 18:36, ICB.

Materials: *governor's palace and jail.*

The priests and teachers had to get the governor to put Jesus to death. So they brought Jesus to Pilate. "Are you the king of the Jews?" Pilate asked. Jesus said yes. "What about all these other bad things the priests and teachers are saying about you?" Pilate asked. But Jesus wouldn't say anything more. Pilate brought Jesus into another room. "Are you a king?" he asked again.

"My kingdom doesn't belong to this world," Jesus said. "I came to show you what God is really like." Pilate talked to Jesus a while longer, then went back to the mob.

"I find nothing wrong with Jesus," he said. "I usually let a prisoner go free at Passover time. You have Jesus here, and Barabbas, a robber who is in jail. Shall I set Jesus free?"

"No!" the crowd shouted. "We want Barabbas!" The priests and teachers and the crowd chose a robber instead of their Saviour and King! How Satan can twist our thinking once we stop listening to Jesus! [Add a palace and jail to your city of Jerusalem. Act out today's story.] ●

#167

Theme: Jesus' Death

"Crucify Him!"

"Look! I am bringing Jesus out to you. I want you to know that I find nothing I can charge against him." John 19:4, ICB.

Materials: *vines, string, paper, glitter, and glue.*

Activity: *weave a crown of vines or green twigs; make a paper crown, adding glitter.*

J esus had done no wrong, but Pilate was scared of the people. So even though Pilate knew Jesus was a good man, he let the soldiers hurt Him. They hit Him and put a crown of thorns on His head. Then Pilate brought Jesus out to the Jews again. But the priests shouted, "Crucify him! He must die because he said he is God's Son!"

Pilate was more afraid than ever. "Where did you come from?" he asked Jesus. He knew the answer. Jesus knew this too, and kept silent. "Do you refuse to speak to me?" Pilate asked. "I have the authority to free you or crucify you."

"You have authority over Me only because God gave it to you," Jesus told him. Pilate wanted to free Jesus, but the crowd wanted Him killed. So finally Pilate gave Jesus to the soldiers to be crucified. Jesus was not only the king of the Jews, He was the king of the universe. You are a child of the King! Jesus deserved a royal crown, but He wore a crown of thorns.

Make a crown of "thorns" and a beautiful crown. ●

Theme: Jesus' Death

#168

King of the Jews

"Father, forgive them. They don't know what they are doing." Luke 23:34, ICB.

Materials: *three crosses stood in clay or sand. A Black man doll or paper cutout for Simon.*

The soldiers put the big, heavy cross on Jesus' back and led Him away to be crucified. But the cross was so heavy that Jesus kept falling. There was a man named Simon in the crowd, and the soldiers told him to carry the cross. Simon was from Cyrene, a town in northern Africa. He was glad to carry the cross for Jesus.

Crowds followed Jesus. Many of the women were crying. "Daughters, don't cry for Me," He said. "Cry for yourselves." Because they did not want Him to be the king in their lives, terrible times would come to them. Jesus' heart ached for them.

When Jesus and two men who were to be crucified with Him reached the place called the Skull, the soldiers set up the three crosses with Jesus in the middle. Even though He was dying, Jesus was thinking of others. "Forgive the soldiers," He begged His Father. "They do not know they are crucifying their Creator."

What a loving, loving Jesus! Act this scene out, using your city of Jerusalem setup. ●

Theme: Jesus' Death

"Remember Me"

"Jesus, remember me when you come into your kingdom!" Luke 23:42, ICB.

Activity: *reenactment.*

Pilate had a sign made to put on Jesus' cross. It said "Jesus of Nazareth: King of the Jews." The priests didn't like the sign. "You should have written 'He said he was king of the Jews,'" they argued. But Pilate wouldn't change it. The priests and soldiers teased Him. "You saved others; save yourself!" But Jesus just hung there—dying for them.

One of the criminals being crucified with Jesus said, "Are you the Messiah? Save yourself and us."

But the man on the other cross said, "Jesus has done no wrong. Jesus, remember me when You come to Your throne." And Jesus promised him, "You will be with Me in Paradise." The first thing that man will see when he wakes up will be Jesus coming with clouds of angels to take him to heaven.

It's not hard to be saved, is it? All you need to do is say, "Save me, Jesus." How wonderful and loving Jesus was, even as He hung on the cross. And He is still the same, loving Saviour today! Act out today's lesson on your set. ●

Theme: Jesus' Death

#170

Jesus' Mother

*They divided my clothes among them,
and they threw lots for my clothing.
Psalm 22:18, ICB.*

Activity: *role-play.*

As Jesus hung on the cross, the soldiers divided His clothes into four piles, one for each soldier. His coat was woven in one piece, so they decided not to cut it up. Instead, they played a game to see who would win Jesus' coat. Jesus was dying for them, but they weren't thinking at all about Him. Only the centurion in charge of the soldiers watched Jesus carefully throughout that long afternoon.

It became dark, even though it was early afternoon. Though the soldiers and priests didn't care, it seemed as though the earth was sad that He was dying. Great clouds covered the sun. The trees twisted in the wind.

Mary, Jesus' mother, stood with John and Jesus' other friends near the cross. "Mother," Jesus said, "depend on John now. He will be your son. And John, treat My mother as your mother now." So John took Mary home with him.

How loving Jesus was to His mother, even as He was dying on the cross! Do you love your mother too? How do you show her how much you love her? [Act out Jesus' final act of care for His mother.] ●

Theme: Jesus' Death

"It Is Finished!"

"My God, my God, why have you left me alone?" Matthew 27:46, ICB.

Materials: *flashlight, material for curtain to rip, toy lamb.*

t had been dark and stormy since noon. Now it was 3:00 in the afternoon, time for the sacrifice of the Passover lamb. The priest had his knife ready to kill the little lamb. But suddenly Jesus cried out, "My God, My God, why have You forsaken Me?" How alone Jesus felt, hanging naked before the world. He was treated as if He were wicked, and Jesus' heart broke. The Father's heart must have hurt even more.

Jesus cried aloud again. "It is finished. Father, into Your hands I commit My spirit."

Then He died. At that very moment the big curtain in the Temple ripped in two. Angels tore it from top to bottom. The priest dropped his knife, and the lamb escaped. Jesus, God's Lamb, had died for the whole world.

The earth shook. Great rocks split open. The centurion who had been watching Jesus was amazed. "This man must have been the Son of God," he said.

[Reenact this story. Turn out lights; light up the cross with flashlight. Rip the curtain in the Temple, and let the lamb escape.] ●

Theme: Jesus' Death

#172

Laid in a Tomb

Then Joseph took the body and wrapped it in a clean linen cloth. Matthew 27:59, ICB.

Materials: *tomb made of oatmeal box and crumpled paper bag.*

A rich man named Joseph had been watching the Crucifixion. He did not like the things done against Jesus. Now Joseph went to Pilate and asked for Jesus' body. Pilate said he could have it. Joseph took Jesus' body down from the cross and wrapped it in a clean linen sheet. Joseph had a new tomb nearby that had been cut out of rock. He brought Jesus' body to this tomb, laid it inside, and rolled a great stone in front of the doorway.

It was almost Sabbath. Everyone went home to rest and keep the Sabbath. Jesus lay in the tomb. He was resting too after His great work of saving the world. He had rested on the Sabbath after making the world. Now He rested again. He had lost the world to Satan. But He had bought us back again, with His own blood.

We already belong to Jesus, because He made us. But we belong to Him again, because He died to save us. What a wonderful God, loving us over and over again, even though we have been so mean to Him! Let's tell Him again how much we love Him. [Make a tomb and act out this part of story.] ●

Theme: Jesus' Death

Jesus Rises From the Grave

"But he is not here. He has risen from death as he said he would."
Matthew 28:6, ICB.

Activity: *role-play.*

It was Sabbath, but the priests and teachers could not rest. They were worried about Jesus, so they went to Pilate. "We remember how Jesus said he would rise again in three days," they said. "His disciples might come and steal him and tell everyone that he was raised from the dead."

So Pilate sent a lot of soldiers to guard the tomb. They were there all Sabbath afternoon and all night. But when it was time for Jesus to rise up, no guard could stop Him. Early Sunday morning there was a violent earthquake. An angel came down from heaven and rolled away the stone. His face shown bright as lightning, and his clothes were as white a snow. The guards shook and fell down like dead men. "Jesus, Your Father calls You," the angel thundered. And Jesus came out of the tomb. The guards ran away.

Meanwhile, two women named Mary were hurrying to the tomb. When they arrived, they saw the angel. "Don't be afraid," the angel said. "Jesus is not here; He has risen."

[Act out these scenes in front of the tomb.] ●

Theme: Resurrection!

#174

MBFJ-24

"I Have Seen the Lord!"

"Woman, why are you crying?"
John 20:13, ICB.

Materials: *figures of Jesus, two angels, Peter and John, two Marys, folded cloths.*

The angel told the women, "Come see the place where Jesus was laid." The women ran to tell Peter and John what they had seen. When Peter and John saw the empty tomb, they finally understood what Jesus had been trying to tell them—that He would die and be raised from the dead.

Mary Magdalene stood near the tomb, crying. Looking inside, she saw two angels who asked why she was crying. "They have taken Jesus away, and I don't know where they have laid Him," she said. Then she turned around and saw a man.

"Whom are you looking for?" (John 20:15, ICB) He asked. "Please tell me where Jesus' body is," Mary said.

Jesus said, "Mary!" Then Mary recognized Him. "Teacher!" she cried.

"Go tell the others that I am going to heaven, to My God and your God," Jesus said.

Mary was bubbling over with joy. She hurried to find Jesus' friends. "I have seen the Lord!" she cried (John 20:18, REB). And then she told them His message. Jesus wouldn't let them forget that after all that had happened He was still their brother. [Act this scene out too.] ●

#175

Theme: Resurrection!

Jesus Appears to His Followers

"Peace be with you!" John 20:19, ICB.

Activity: *running in the dark.*

Mary had seen Jesus; Peter and John had seen the empty tomb. But Jesus' other friends couldn't believe He was alive. The city was full of stories. Soldiers said that Jesus' body had been stolen. Jesus' friends were afraid, so they hid behind locked doors. And two of Jesus' friends were hurrying home to Emmaus, a little town not far from Jerusalem. They felt confused. Why had Jesus let Himself be killed?

Jesus came up and started walking with them, but they didn't recognize Him. Then He explained the Scriptures to them, how He was supposed to come to this earth and die. When the men were home, they invited the stranger to eat with them. So Jesus sat down at the table. He took the bread and said the blessing. Suddenly they saw that it was Jesus!

In that moment Jesus disappeared. His two friends jumped up and ran seven miles in the dark all the way back to Jerusalem. They could hardly wait to tell their friends Jesus was really alive! [Carefully, run in the dark. Say as you run, "Jesus is alive. He is risen."] ●

Theme: Resurrection!

#176

It Is Really Jesus!

"You saw these things happen—you are witnesses. You must tell people to change their hearts and lives." Luke 24:47, ICB.

Materials: *four paper plates, markers, glue, string.*

Activity: *Glue two plates face-to-face. Draw features of earth. On other plates draw around hands and wrists. Cut out. Glue to bottom of globe, encircling. Hang with string.*

I t was Sunday evening, the day that Jesus had risen from the dead. [Review who had seen Jesus since then.] Jesus' disciples were excited. "It's true!" they exclaimed. "He has appeared to Simon Peter!" The two men who'd run back from Emmaus told how Jesus had walked and talked with them. "Our hearts were on fire as He explained Scripture to us!" Suddenly Jesus stood in the middle of the group. His friends were terrified. They thought Jesus was a ghost! "Why are you so scared?" Jesus asked. "Touch Me.

Ghosts don't have flesh and bones as I have. Do you have anything to eat?" Jesus took a piece of fish and ate it to show He was real.

Then Jesus said, "Now you can see what I was talking about in the Scriptures. Moses and the prophets said that the Messiah would die, and be raised on the third day. From now on, people all over the world may ask forgiveness for their sins in My name. Go to people all over the world and tell them I will save them from their sins!"

Make a globe to remind you that Jesus saves the whole world. ●

Theme: Resurrection!

"My Lord and My God!"

But these are written that you can believe that Jesus is the Christ, the Son of God. John 20:31, ICB.

Materials: *black felt, white felt, small pictures of Bible stories, fabric marker, tacky or hot glue.*

Everyone but Jesus' friend Thomas had seen Jesus. The others told him, "Jesus is alive!" But Thomas wouldn't believe them. "Unless I see the mark of the nails on His hands I will not believe." A week later Thomas and some friends were in the room together. They'd locked the door because they were still afraid. Suddenly they saw Jesus. He said, "Peace be with you!" Jesus never wants us to ever be afraid. He looked kindly at Thomas. "Look at My hands, and touch them," He said. "Believe I am really alive."

Thomas fell on his knees. "My Lord and my God!" (John 20:28, REB).

Jesus said, "You believe Me because you have seen Me. Other people will believe in Me, even though they haven't seen Me."

We believe in Jesus, even though we haven't seen Him. We read the Bible stories about Him so we can know Him better.

Make a felt Bible. Cut out a seven-by-ten-inch piece of black felt for the cover; write "Holy Bible" on it. Cut out a six-by-nine-inch piece of white felt for the pages. Sew or staple the pages inside the cover. Glue pictures of Jesus' stories on the pages. ●

Theme: Faith

#178

Breakfast on the Beach

They knew it was the Lord.
John 21:12, ICB.

Activity: *fixing a breakfast tray.*

Several of Jesus' friends rowed out into the lake just as it was getting dark. They fished all night, but didn't catch a single fish. Early in the morning a Man called to them from the shore. "Friends, have you caught anything?" But they hadn't. "Throw the net out to starboard, and you'll make a catch."

They'd been fishing from the left side. Now they threw the nets out of the right side of the boat. Suddenly so many fish filled the net that they couldn't pull it in!

Jesus was the only one who could do that! Peter jumped overboard and swam to where Jesus was standing on the beach. The others rowed the boat to the beach, towing the net full of fish. Jesus was cooking fish on a fire. "Bring your fish and have breakfast," He said. (There were 153 big fish in the net.) Jesus served them the fish He'd cooked and the bread He had ready.

What a cozy time they must have had around the fire that early morning on the beach.

Have you ever fixed breakfast for someone you love? Try it soon. ●

#179

Theme: Jesus' Love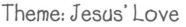

Coming Again

"You saw Jesus taken away from you into heaven. He will come back in the same way you saw him go." Acts 1:11, ICB.

Materials: *cotton balls, pictures of angels, Jesus on His throne, glitter.*

Jesus stayed with His friends for a while, then His friends watched Him go up into the sky until a cloud of angels hid Him from sight. As they were trying to catch their last glimpse of Jesus, two men dressed in white came to stand beside them. "Why are you standing here, looking up into the sky?" they asked. "This same Jesus will come back again in the very same way you saw Him go into heaven."

Soon Jesus will come back in all His glory and we'll meet Him in the air. I can hardly wait! Jesus is in heaven right now, getting ready for us to come live with Him. He's getting our homes ready, and that supper that He promised to eat with us in heaven. The angels are eager to come too, to take us home to heaven. Are you getting ready to go with Him? I am!

Make a picture of Jesus coming with all His angels to take us to live with Him. [Or hang up the one you made in lesson 154.] Take several days to draw pictures of your beautiful homes. And don't forget the big supper table!

Theme: Second Coming ✂ ❀

#180

Index 1

2 x 2 cloth (71)
3 x 5 cards (27)
4 x 6 cards (59-64)
8½ x 11 white paper (7)

angels (180)
apron (133)

baby doll (2)
Baby Jesus and manger (2)
bank (153)
basin of water (6, 159)
basket (8, 91, 111)
beans (65)
bear, miniature (71)
Bible (8)
Bible story books (8, 178)
Bible story characters (19, 178)
blanket (152)
blessings scrapbook (12-19)
blindfold (53, 74)
blocks (39, 42, 47, 91)

boat (112)
bottled spring water (57)
bowl (8, 21)
bows (3, 28, 160)
branches (134, 136)
bread (52, 61, 111)
bread recipe (106)
buttons (75, 139)

camel (129)
can with lid (to bury) (107)
candle (21, 53, 89)
car (5, 39)
cardboard bed (47)
cardboard box (2, 42, 66)
cardboard tubes (9, 86, 87, 120)
cardboard wreath (97)
cards and envelopes (142)
cheese (111)
child picture (103)
child's photo (63, 121)
children's quarterly (97)
clear plastic cups (99-102)
cloth scraps (2, 172, 175)
clothespins (77)

Note: *Check these lists for items you may need to save, borrow, or purchase. Check the specific devotional if you question whether you really need each item called for. You may be able to substitute another item you already have. (The devotional reading for which an item will be used appears in parentheses following the item.)*

M a t e r i a l s   L i s t

coins (144)
contact paper (121)
cookie (74)
cotton balls (66, 77, 160, 172, 180)
crackers (161)
craft foam (92)
crayons (113, 144)
crime, war, disaster (15)
cross (three) (169)
cup (72, 98-101)

dirt (5, 98)
doll (black man, or cardboard cutout) (169)
doll house (96, 97)
dolls–children, parents, grandparents,
    Barbie and Ken (6, 37, 38, 47, 112,
    116, 164-175)
door (36)
dress-up clothes (26)
dried grass (2)
dry food items (72)

earth (14, 115)
empty oatmeal box (173)

fabric markers or puffy paint (92, 149, 178)
fake pearls/gems (108)
family photographs (97)
feathers (33)

felt (33, 92, 95, 139, 149, 178)
figure of Jesus (can be Ken doll) (66)
fire (165)
flashlight (10, 172)
flour (110)
flowers (88)
fruit, fruit trees (40)
fruit, vegetables (40)

gift (36)
gift box (160)
glitter (59, 64, 73, 168, 180)
globe (115)
glue (15, 16, 20, 55, 59, 64, 67, 69, 87, 97,
    115, 141, 147, 168, 177)
gold stars (38)
grain (71)
grape juice (161)
grapevine (54)
grass (89)

hair clips (80)
heart, dirty, white, red (17)
happy face stickers (19)
heart stickers (62, 73, 98-100)
heavy paper/cardboard (31, 33, 56, 77)
hole punch (1)
iron-on fabric (133)

Materials List

Jesus (12, 18, 44, 46, 56, 66, 85, 95, 96, 160, 180)

lace (88)
lamb, miniature (160, 172)
lamp (10, 21)
large bowl (8)
large handkerchief (74, 75, 134)

markers (1, 9, 16, 22, 23, 27, 28, 33, 38, 43, 44, 45, 59, 63, 64, 75, 80, 102, 103, 117, 124, 177)
matches (21, 89)
metal decorative studs (30)
money (108, 166)

National Geographic magazines (97)
needle/thread (75, 129)
New Jerusalem (60)
notebook (78, 157)
note writing materials (109, 142)

oil (72, 110, 156)
oil lamp (156)
old Christmas cards (1)
old sheet (154)

paint (30, 154)
paper (16, 20, 22, 23, 28, 43, 44, 45, 49, 62, 63, 67, 69, 70, 83, 84, 86, 87, 88, 102, 108, 113, 115, 117, 122, 124, 129, 138, 141, 145, 147, 168)
paper, crumpled (173)
paper, stiff (9)
paper or sheet for mural (154)
paper doilies (88)
paper fasteners (131)
paper plates (126, 131, 177)
party balloons, hats, etc. (143)
paste (12, 22)
pen (126)
pencils (7, 16, 49, 78, 83, 113, 122, 130)
people (12, 13, 14, 37, 39, 97)
perfume (76)
pictures from cards/magazines (121)
pinking shears (95)
pipe cleaners (yellow) (70)
plant (58)
popsicle sticks (140)
potato (90)
potting soil (101)

rags (85, 139)
rainbow (73)
real flowers (34)
reed (89)
ribbons (3, 18, 52, 160)
robes (50, 51)

rocks (5, 65, 68)
roll of paper (90, 117, 154)
rooster, miniature (165)

Sabbath school mission reports (153)
sad pictures (15)
safety pins (95, 149)
salt (20, 110)
sand (42)
scarf (134)
scenery (67)
scissors (3, 9, 12, 63, 84, 92, 97, 117, 122, 126, 145, 147)
scrapbook (12-19)
seeds (98-101)
shoe box (66-73, 164)
sign (heaven) (41)
small cardboard boxes (3, 28, 30, 160)
socks (139)
songbooks (8)
spade (107)
sponge (59, 68, 154)
spoons (36)
sticks (65, 70, 82, 160)
storytelling cards (cards that tell a story in sequence) (79)
string (47, 82, 85, 122, 133, 168, 177)
Styrofoam ball (55)
sunglasses (31)

table, miniature (96)
tacky glue (33, 95, 178)
tape (3, 18, 30, 90, 122)
tape player or video maker (93, 94)
tea towel (8)
tempera paint (90)
thistles (100)
thread (52, 133)
tissue paper, all colors (55)
toothbrush, paste (74)
towel (105, 133, 159)
toys (24, 26, 91)
translucent paper (31)
treasure (107)
trumpet (154)
typing paper (144)
twigs (68, 70, 82, 89)

vines (168)

weedy soil (100)
whole egg shells (33)
wolf, miniature (71)
wood scraps (35)
wrapping paper (3, 160)

yarn (1, 9, 44, 86, 87, 139)
your child's picture (63, 104, 121)

Materials List

Index 2

FAMILY OR DOLL PUPPET ACTIVITIES

(See directions in devotional 139)
arguing (119, 139)
being kind (158)
forgiveness (125)
Jesus at dinnertime (97)
problem-solving (123)

Index 3

ACTIVITIES AND GAMES

baptism (6)
blindfold (74)
body, fingerplay (45, 105)
breakfast on the beach (179)
building on sand (39, 42)
buried treasure (107)
directions (118)
dishwashing (151)
finding flowers (34)
growing like a seed (104, 105)
hide-and-seek (4, 36)
jumping (131)
listening game (118)
lost sheep (65)
making crowns (168)
making fish (120)
matching (40)
mother says (32)
neighborhood trip (127)
paths in dirt (5)
Peter's story (165)
picnic (111)
planting (99-102)
praise with branches (134, 136)
puppets (75, 123, 125, 138, 158)
race (155, 176)
raking leaves (91)
reenactment (164, 170)
role-play (49, 81, 119, 123, 125, 135, 140, 146, 158, 163, 171, 174)
running in dark (176)
secret helper (148)
shadows (10)
singing (11, 29, 136)
something special (162)
storytelling (79)
trumpet playing (154)
values, list (150)
visiting a spring (57)
walk (25, 78, 116)
walking blindfolded (74)
watching thunderstorm (154)

whisper, shout (79)
withered plant (137)

Index 4

THEMES

angels (122, 176)
animals (27, 33, 114, 152, 165)
arguing (139)

baptism (6, 7)
being fair (131)
Bible (8, 178)
blessings (72)
bread (8, 52, 106)
breakfast on the beach (179)
building on sand (39, 42)

candles (21, 53, 89)
choosing (39)
church (135)
clothes (34)
cross (82, 85)
crown (168)

death (51, 58)
directions (118)
doors, gates (36, 39, 56, 97)

faith (44, 114, 119, 138, 178)
fairness (137)
finding flowers (34)

growing like a seed (104, 105)

lost sheep (65)

matching garden foods (40)
mother says (32)

neighborhood trip (127)

paths in dirt (5)
picnic (111)
planting (99-102)

raking leaves (91)
role playing (49, 81, 119, 123, 125, 135,
    140, 146, 158, 163, 171, 174)
running in dark (176)

values, list (150)
visiting a spring (57)

walk (25, 78, 116)
walking blindfolded (74)
withered plant (137)

Index 5

scripture

Psalms

22:18 171
23:1 66
23:2 67
23:3 . . . . . . 68, 69
23:4 70
23:5 . . . . . . 71, 72
23:6 73

Malachi

4:2 55

Matthew

1:21 1
2:11 3
3:3 5
3:11 6
3:17 7
4:4 8
4:16 10
4:19 9
4:23 11
5:3 12
5:4 13
5:5 14
5:6 15
5:7 16
5:8 17
5:9 18
5:10 19
5:13 20
5:14 21
5:22 22
5:37 23
5:39 24
5:42 25
5:44 27
5:48 28
6:8 29
6:9 59
6:10 60
6:11 61
6:12 62
6:13 . . . . . . 63, 64
6:21 30
6:22 31
6:24 32
6:26 33
6:28 34
7:1 35
7:7 36
7:9 37
7:12 38
7:13 39
7:16 40
7:21 41
7:24 42
8:2, 3 43
8:8 44
8:26 . . . . . . 45, 46
9:9 48
9:13 49
9:22 50
9:24 51
9:36 77
10:8 78
10:26 79
10:30 80
10:32 81
10:38 82
10:42 83
11:15 84
11:28 85
12:8 86
12:12 87
12:18 88
12:19 89
12:25 90
12:30 91
12:32 92
12:34 93
12:36 94
12:41 95
12:50 97
13:4 98
13:20 99
13:22 100
13:23 101
13:24 102
13:31 104
13:32 105
13:33 106
13:43 103
13:44 107
13:45 108
13:57 109
14:18 110
14:20 111
14:27 112
15:4 113
15:25 114
15:28 115
16:2 116
16:24 117
17:5 118
17:20 119
17:27 120
18:3 121
18:10 122
18:15 123
18:22 124
18:27 125

19:14 126
19:21 . . . . . 127, 128
19:26 129
20:16 131
20:19 132
20:26 133
20:28 130
20:33 74
21:2 134
21:13 135
21:15 136
21:20 137
21:21 138
21:23 139
21:28 140
21:33 141
22:14 . . . . . 142, 143
22:21 144
22:37 145

22:39 . . . . . 146, 147
23:12 149
`23:16 148
23:23 150
23:25 151
23:37 152
24:14 153
24:27 154
24:42 155
25:13 156
25:21 157
25:31 158
26:29 161
26:41 162
26:45 163
26:63 164
26:73 165
27:5 166
27:46 172

27:59 173
28:6 174

Luke

2:7 2
2:46 4
5:24 47
6:30 26
7:37 76
13:12 75
15:6 65
23:34 169
23:42 170
24:47 177

John

3:16 160
4:14 57
6:35 52
8:12 53

10:7 56
11:25 58
13:14 159
15:5 54
18:36 167
19:4 168
20:13 175
20:19 176
20:31 178
21:12 179

Acts
1:11 180

Revelation
3:20 96